1977.

Hull Conference.

THE TEXT OF THE NEW TESTAMENT

THE TEXT OF THE NEW TESTAMENT

A Short Introduction

BY

VINCENT TAYLOR

Ph.D., D.D. (London), Hon. D.D. (Leeds),
Hon. D.D. (Dublin), Hon. D.D. (Glasgow), F.B.A.

SECOND EDITION

LONDON
MACMILLAN & CO LTD
NEW YORK · ST MARTIN'S PRESS
1963

MACMILLAN AND COMPANY LIMITED
St Martin's Street London WC2
also Bombay Calcutta Madras Melbourne

THE MACMILLAN COMPANY OF CANADA LIMITED
Toronto

ST MARTIN'S PRESS INC
New York

PRINTED IN GREAT BRITAIN

PREFACE TO THE SECOND EDITION

I HAVE carefully revised the first edition of the present work and have taken the opportunity to make a few corrections and additions. Page 4 has been rewritten. In its original form it was too much compressed and did not give sufficient attention to the genealogical argument of Westcott and Hort to which reference is also made on page 50. I have also added a note on page 7 which explains more fully the use of the symbols $\alpha \beta \gamma \delta$. I have added a reference to P^{75}, some account of which is given by Professor B. M. Metzger in the *Expository Times* for April 1962, and have inserted this MS in the ' Notes on Select Readings ' relating to Lk. xxii, 19b–20, 43 f, xxiii. 34a, Jn. i. 18, v. 3b–4, and vii. 53–viii. 11.

I take the opportunity of emphasizing again that the book is not a rival of the classical works of Lake and Kenyon, but an introduction to these and other works for the benefit of beginners in this fascinating but difficult subject.

VINCENT TAYLOR

PREFACE TO THE FIRST EDITION

THIS book is intended to be a short introduction to the textual criticism of the New Testament. There is, I believe, need for a work of this kind to provide preliminary studies leading to the classic discussions of Westcott and Hort, F. G. Kenyon, A. Souter, K. Lake, and B. H. Streeter. It is based on a lifetime's study of the subject and many years' experience of teaching in this field. Many teachers feel far from satisfied with the results of their labours and are concerned at the failure of so many students to carry their interest beyond the classroom and the demands of examination syllabuses. Many students find the subject irksome and are glad to put it aside as soon as possible, while others find a fascinating interest in it which, none the less, is not easy to sustain, with the result that experts in textual criticism are surprisingly few. F. G. Kenyon refers to this situation in his stimulating work, *Recent Developments in the Textual Criticism of the Greek Bible*. 'It is very regrettable,' he writes, 'that the textual criticism of the New Testament does not appear to appeal to the younger generation of scholars so strongly as it did to their predecessors in the nineteenth century'. He regrets that there seem to be 'lamentably few' who are carrying on the tradition of Lachmann and Tregelles and Tischendorf and Hort and Scrivener and Wordsworth and others of the earlier generation, in spite of the fascination of the subject and the fact that much good work remains to be done. F. C. Burkitt made a similar lament in his *Christian Beginnings* in 1924, although in his case the regrets extended to historical criticism in general.

'Alas,' Burkitt wrote, 'the old interest is dying.' Those who still believe in Religion, he declared, tend more and more to rely on 'Experience', and he affirmed that this was the case with Neo-Catholicism almost as much as with Methodism and other Protestant varieties of religion. 'From the scientific, academical, point of view,' he continues, 'this means that Psychology gains and Historical Criticism loses. The bright, intelligent young man, whose interest in Religion has kept him from becoming an engineer or a geologist, now tends to take up the Philosophy of Religion with Psychology. . . . In the next generation I fear there will be fewer investigators still who are occupied with the past.' Burkitt's prophecy has proved to be true. Indeed the process has been accelerated by the competing claims of Typology and Biblical Theology. These new interests, especially those of Biblical Theology, are not to be lamented, but the consequences to Textual Criticism have proved disastrous.

Teachers of Textual Criticism, however, must be honest enough to admit their own responsibilities. At least two aspects of the situation must be recognized. The student has been encouraged, or has felt himself obliged if he is serious, to commit to memory too many facts concerning manuscripts and versions, and secondly he has not given sufficient attention to practical, as distinguished from theoretical, work, with the result that he felt himself overwhelmed with a mass of detail which the expert carries with a light heart. All who have practical experience as examiners will have noticed that questions about the interpretation of textual readings tend to be avoided, or when such questions are compulsory, to be answered perfunctorily. It has not been sufficiently recognized that the intelligent interest of the subject, as well as its practical importance, lies just in the elucidation of the data given in an *apparatus criticus*, and the student finds it hard to believe that it is in the study of textual notes that he acquires theoretical knowledge almost unawares. The situation is precisely like that which obtains in engineering and the physical sciences. The young engineer who faces and accomplishes practical tasks obtains a knowledge of detail which is almost unbelievable, and the same is true of the scientist. *Mutatis mutandis*, the same is true also of textual criticism, a fact which doubtless explains the irritating opinion of the expert that his subject is an easy option.

It may be objected that I have directed the reader's attention in the first place to eight uncial MSS only, with a dozen or more to be memorized later, and to a comparatively small number of papyrus MSS, minuscules, and Old Latin and Vulgate MSS. This minimum requirement is adopted deliberately because, with this knowledge and the application of the principles of textual criticism, a beginning of the study of readings can be made almost at once, and this is important because, as explained above, textual studies increase familiarity with the mass of necessary detail rapidly. The method adopted might be called textual criticism without tears. The description, however, is too negative since the method quickly stimulates interest so that the subject becomes a pleasure, not a thing of drudgery.

In pursuance of this aim I have added an unusual number of notes on Select Readings in Chapter XII, with comments and references to notable discussions. These Notes are meant to be studied and not merely read. I have not supplied a full list of MSS because such lists are readily available in G. D. Kilpatrick's edition of the British and Foreign Bible Society's text, in B. H. Streeter's *Four Gospels*, and the second edition of A. H. M'Neile's *An Introduction to the Study of the New Testament* edited by C. S. C. Williams.

It remains only to emphasize the importance of this discipline. How can we study the history of doctrine with profit unless we have not only an accurate text, but the ability to see why it is accurate, and at the same time have the knowledge to distinguish between variant readings?

More important is the personal discovery of the close connexion between the text and the history of the ancient Church in the harmonization of parallel readings, the influence of the Old Testament and liturgical formulae upon the New Testament, and the manner in which devotion and doctrine have reacted upon its form. It is important also that in literary and historical criticism, of which textual criticism is an essential part, a special field should be investigated in which decisions must be taken and judgements formed on the solid basis of facts supplied by the manuscript tradition. A habit of mind is thereby formed which is of the greatest value when more speculative problems have to be faced. Most of all, textual criticism has an appeal all its own because in it we can have the conviction that we are approaching nearer to the original autographs of the New Testament which it has pleased God not to protect from the accidents and fortunes of scribal transmission.

I desire gratefully to acknowledge the generous help I have received from my former student and colleague, the Rev. Owen E. Evans, M.A., B.D., now Tutor in New Testament Language and Literature at Hartley Victoria College, Manchester, in the correction of the proofs. I am also much indebted to the accuracy of the printers and readers on the staff of Messrs. MacLehose, of the University Press, Glasgow, in the setting of the type, which is always a difficult undertaking in the case of a work on Textual Criticism. For the final result I am myself responsible and I hope that readers will find the work useful and stimulating.

VINCENT TAYLOR

ABBREVIATIONS

CONTENTS

BIBLIOGRAPHY

F. C. Burkitt, 'Text and Versions', article, *Encyclopaedia Biblica*, iv, cols. 4977–5031 (1907). *Evangelion da-Mepharreshe*, ii (1904).

A. C. Clark, *The Primitive Text of the Gospels and Acts*, (1914). *The Acts of the Apostles* (1933).

E. C. Colwell and D. W. Riddle, *Prolegomena to the Study of the Lectionary Text of the Gospels*, i (1933).

C. R. Gregory, *Tischendorf's Novum Testamentum Graece*, 8th ed., iii, *Prolegomena* (1884).

F. G. Kenyon, *Handbook to the Textual Criticism of the New Testament*, 2nd ed. (1926). *Recent Developments in the Textual Criticism of the Greek Bible* (1933). Cited as 'Recent Developments'. *The Text of the Greek Bible* (1937). *Our Bible and the Ancient Manuscripts*, 4th ed. (1933).

M.-J. Lagrange, *Introduction à l'étude du Nouveau Testament: deuxième partie: critique textuelle, II La Critique rationelle* (1935).

K. Lake, *The Text of the New Testament*, 6th ed. (1928).

K. Lake, R. P. Blake and S. New, *Harvard Theological Review*, xxi, 4 (1928), 208–404.

A. T. Robertson, *Textual Criticism of the New Testament* (1925).

J. H. Ropes, 'The Text of the Acts of the Apostles', *The Beginnings of Christianity*, ed. F. J. F. Jackson and K. Lake, iii, *The Text*, (1926).

A. Souter, *The Text and Canon of the New Testament* (1954), 2nd ed. edited by C. S. C. Williams.

B. H. Streeter, *The Four Gospels* (1924).

A. Vaganay, *An Introduction to the Textual Criticism of the New Testament* (tr. B. V. Miller), (1937).

B. F. Westcott and F. J. A. Hort, *The New Testament in Greek, II, Introduction* (1896).

A. Wikenhauser, *New Testament Introduction* (Eng. Tr. 1958), pp. 62–149.

C. S. C. Williams, *Alterations to the Text of the Synoptic Gospels and Acts* (1951). Cited as 'Alterations'. The 2nd edition of A. H. M'Neile's *Introduction to the New Testament* (1953) pp. 373–453.

I

THE PURPOSE AND METHODS OF TEXTUAL CRITICISM

THE object of Textual Criticism is to recover, as far as possible, the original text of the New Testament writings. The need arises from the many corruptions which crept into the text during the long period when copies were made by hand, that is until the discovery of printing about A.D. 1450. The difficulty of copying a letter or document is well known. In spite of the best intentions in the world we often read the text amiss and write what is in our own mind, or for various reasons, some of which are mentioned below, we may omit words and phrases which are in the original. Textual criticism is necessary in the case of all ancient writings, including the ancient Classics; but it is especially necessary for the New Testament in view of its supreme value for the Church and the individual reader.

The task is difficult. As regards the New Testament it is occasioned by the great wealth of the manuscript tradition. In contrast with the Gospels and Epistles some of the ancient Latin and Greek Classics are represented by comparatively few manuscripts, and these are for the most part late in date. For the plays of Aeschylus some fifty MSS are available and for those of Sophocles about a hundred MSS, and this means that sometimes the original text is irretrievably lost and has to be represented by conjecture. For the New Testament over 4,000 Greek MSS exist: there are also some 8,000 MSS of the Latin Vulgate, and at least 1,000 of other versions into which the original books were translated. In short, some 13,000 MSS of parts of the New Testament are available, and, what is more significant, no two of them agree in every detail. This fact alone suggests that, while the Scriptures are inspired, they are not verbally inspired: otherwise it is difficult to think that so great a disparity would exist.

The task of Textual Criticism is difficult, but it is not impossible. If we possessed only a few MSS, the original readings might in many cases be completely lost, and recoverable only by guesswork. As it is, the very large number of MSS actually gives greater promise of success, since it is highly probable that the original text exists somewhere, if by the use of the right methods it can be found. Moreover, many New Testament MSS stand appreciably nearer to the original writings, or the autographs as they are called, than do the MSS of the Classics.

What then are the methods adopted by the textual critic?

First, he must, as far as possible, correct individual MSS and attempt to estimate their value. He must seek to eliminate errors of two kinds, unintentional and intentional.

Unintentional errors arise by accident and through overstrain and preoccupation on the part of the copyist. They are defined as follows.

1. *Itacism.* This term is used to describe wrong spelling or grammar. For example, ποισαι may be written instead of ποιῆσαι. The traditional term is not a good one, but it is used because the vowel *iota* is often involved.

2. *Haplography.* This is the mistake of writing a word once when the original has it twice. Thus, κυριε may be written for κυριε, κυριε.

3. *Dittography.* This term describes the opposite mistake of writing a word or phrase twice when it should be copied once. The text-books usually give as an example the reading of the Laudian MS (E₂) in Ac. ii. 4, *et repleti sunt et repleti sunt omnes spiritu sancto.*

4. *Homoioteleuton.* This long word is used for the omission of words and phrases because they end and sound alike. For example, Jn. xvii. 15 reads οὐκ ἐρωτῶ ἵνα ἄρῃς αὐτοὺς ἐκ τοῦ κόσμου ἀλλ᾿ ἵνα τηρήσῃς αὐτοὺς ἐκ τοῦ πονηροῦ. In Codex Vaticanus (B) the scribe's eye manifestly passed from the first ἐκ τοῦ to the second with the result that the intervening words were omitted. Such an error often happens in the process of typewriting.

Intentional errors arise because with the best will in the world the scribe seeks to amend the text which he has before him. They include:

1. *Marginal Notes* which may be transferred to the text.

2. *Traditional Readings* wanting in the document copied may be inserted.

3. *Grammatical Improvements* may be made. For example the indicative may be replaced by the subjunctive. This may well be the case in Rom. v. 1, where most MSS read ἔχωμεν instead of ἔχομεν.

4. *Harmonistic Alterations* frequently arise when the scribe in copying the text of a particular Gospel inserts a reading familiar to him from his knowledge of a different Gospel.

5. *Dogmatic Alterations.* These are made when the scribe alters the text he is copying in the interest of doctrine. This kind of error is certainly present in the different forms in which Mt. i. 16 (the end of the Matthaean Genealogy) appears in Greek, Latin, and Syriac MSS. The examples are not difficult to detect, although naturally there may be differences of opinion in different cases. For a study of this fascinating question the student may be referred to C. S. C. Williams' short but valuable work, *Alterations to the Text of the Synoptic Gospels and Acts* (1951).

The question necessarily arises: How is the critic to decide between different readings present in the manuscript tradition?

(1) A principle of considerable importance in judging variant readings is one laid down by the great textual critic J. A. Bengel (1687–1752), namely, that the harder reading is to be preferred (*Difficilior lectio potior*). For example, the reading of Codex D in Mk. i. 41, 'being angry', is much more difficult than the reading 'being moved with compassion' attested by almost all other MSS, and is more likely to be original. (See page 82 f.) Cf. *NEB*, 'in warm indignation'. This principle is generally sound in relation to intentional errors, but is not necessarily valid in the case of unintentional or accidental alterations, for these may be so difficult as not to make good sense.

(2) A better principle, adopted by modern textual critics, is: of two or more alternative readings, that one is more likely to be right which accounts for the origin of the others. A good example is Mk. iv. 28, πλήρης σῖτον (Codex Ephraemi), in which the adjective is an indeclinable. Apparently, this was forgotten, and πλῆρες σῖτος (Vaticanus) and πλήρης ὁ σῖτος (Bezae) are grammatical corrections. So also the common reading πλήρη σῖτον.

(3) Opinions may differ as to whether a particular reading accounts for other variants, and it is the service of Hort (see page 50) that he has shown the importance of *genealogy*. By observing errors common to a group of MSS it is reasonable to conclude that the MSS are descendants of a common ancestor, and so belong to a distinct family. A family is a group of MSS marked by distinctive characteristics and often connected with a particular locality like the members of a genealogical tree. The character of the family stamps the worth of its members. B. H. Streeter (as we shall see) has insisted that MSS should be weighed, not counted. 'The weight of a MS', he writes, 'depends on the extent to which it preserves, more or less, one of the ancient local texts.'[1]

[1] *The Four Gospels*, p. 107. See further, chapter xi.

II

NOTATION AND TYPES OF TEXT

NOTATION. It is important at the outset to become familiar with the signs by which MSS are denoted. The signs consist of letters from the Latin, Greek, and Hebrew alphabets, both capital and small letters, and of Arabic numerals. The earlier systems were both complicated and ambiguous, the same letters and numbers being used in some cases to denote different MSS in the Gospels, the Acts and Catholic Epistles, the Pauline Epistles and the Apocalypse. In his critical edition of the New Testament (1902–13) H. von Soden devised a new and ingenious method, in which all MSS are indicated by numerals preceded by the symbols δ (those containing the entire New Testament with or without the Apocalypse), ε (those containing the Gospels), and α (those of the Acts and Epistles, again with or without the Apocalypse). The numerals are so arranged as to indicate the date and the contents of the MS in question, and the MSS are grouped under the symbols K, H, and I, according to the type of text (see below) they represent.

Von Soden's system, while still in use, is exceedingly complicated and the chronological information and the indication of types are uncertain. Accordingly, in 1908 C. R. Gregory, after consultation with leading textual critics, produced a list which has been widely adopted and is now in general use.[1] Gregory's revised system is as follows:

1. *Papyrus MSS* are denoted by the symbol P with numbers in the right-hand top corner (e.g. P[13]).

[1] Cf. *Die griechischen Handschriften des Neuen Testaments* (1908).

2. *Uncial Greek MSS*[1] are indicated by Latin and Greek capital letters, Hebrew characters being abandoned, except ℵ for Codex Sinaiticus. The same letter is not used for different MSS (except D_2, E_2, H_3, and a few others). Other MSS are denoted by numbers in Clarendon type (046, etc.).

3. *Minuscule MSS*[2] are denoted by numbers in ordinary type and there is only one series instead of four. Formerly different MSS might be represented by the same number in the Gospels, the Acts and Catholic Epistles, the Pauline Epistles, and the Apocalypse.

4. *The Old Latin Version*: The MSS are denoted by the small letters of the Latin Alphabet (a, b, c, etc.).

The advantages of Gregory's system are that it is simple, workable, and makes the least possible break with the old notation. The symbols for other Versions will be found in the sections where these MSS are treated.[3]

Other Abbreviations. The following are widely used.

pc (*pauci*) = a few other MSS.

al (*alii*) = other MSS, a greater number.

pm (*permulti*) = most other MSS.

pl (*plerique*) = most MSS or very many. So also ω used by Souter.

rell (*reliqui*) = the remaining witnesses.

TYPES OF TEXT. By a type of text is meant the Greek text as it was commonly read at a particular time or place, or even in a definite group of MSS. Such a type would be brought into existence by the accidents of scribal transmission, intentional and unintentional. It will be useful to indicate the principal types of text described by Westcott and Hort, although their textual theory remains to be explained and discussed.[4] The types are as follows:

1. *The α Text.* By this is meant the Greek text as it was almost universally read from the fourth century onwards.

---

[1] See later, pp. 15–22.   [2] See later, pp. 23–6.
[3] See pp. 27–38.   [4] See pp. 49–56.

Westcott and Hort call it the Syrian or Antiochian text; Streeter's name is the Byzantian text.

2. *The β Text.* That is, the text represented by Codex Vaticanus (B) and its allies. Westcott and Hort's name is the Neutral Text; Streeter's the Alexandrian Text.

3. *The γ Text.* This, in Westcott and Hort's view, is a revised form of the β text, to which they gave the name Alexandrian. Streeter treats it as a mere refinement of the β text, and does not distinguish it as a separate text.

4. *The δ Text.* This is the text of Codex Bezae (D) and its allies, the Old Latin version and (formerly) the Old Syriac version. The name 'Western' Text, given to it by Westcott and Hort, is a misnomer, since the Old Syriac is an eastern text. The 'Western' Text was current from the second century onwards and was regarded by Westcott and Hort as a corrupt text. For more than a generation its value and importance have been steadily rising in critical opinion. Streeter[1] suggested that it should be divided into a Western proper and an Eastern text. Under the former he distinguished the texts of Italy and Gaul and of Carthage, and under the latter the texts of Antioch and Caesarea. These hypotheses will be discussed in detail later.

Note. The symbols α β γ δ are used by Westcott and Hort chronologically. Thus, in their usage, α denotes the text of B and its allies, β the text of D, γ the 'Alexandrian' text, and δ the late ecclesiastical text of A and its allies. The usage of Kenyon (*Handbook*, 1901, and *The Text of the Greek Bible*, 1937) is much to be preferred, since the symbols (except γ) correspond with A, B and D.

[1] *The Four Gospels*, 64–76.

III

THE PAPYRUS PERIOD

THE period during which the New Testament MSS were written upon papyrus material extended from about A.D. 50 to the beginning of the fourth century. It is important because the original writings or autographs were written on this material and to this period our earliest MSS belong. It is true that skins had been used for synagogue books, but the New Testament writings were at first regarded as ordinary books, and so would be written on papyrus material. Skins were too cumbrous and vellum did not come into use until the fourth century. The general character and appearance of the autographs are illustrated by the papyri which have been discovered in the sands of Egypt.

Papyrus Material. Papyrus writing material was formed from dried strips of the papyrus plant which grew in profusion in the valley of the Nile. The strips were first laid side by side vertically and other strips were superimposed horizontally. Fastened together by Nile water and glue they were then subjected to pressure and the surface was smoothed and made serviceable for writing. The horizontal side was known as the *Recto* and the vertical side, normally left blank, as the *Verso*. Sometimes both sides were used, and this is the explanation of the description of the roll mentioned in Ezek. ii. 10 as 'written within and without' and of the book described in Apoc. v. 1 as 'written within and on the back'. The sheets of writing material obtained in this way varied in height from 6 to over 15 inches and in width from 3 to 9 inches.

The Roll Form. The next stage in the making of an ancient

book was to fasten sheets together to form a roll. The roll might be of any convenient length, but normally did not exceed 32 to 35 feet. A single sheet 11 by 6 inches would be enough for the transcribing of 2 and 3 John in a single column, but for Romans a roll 11 feet 6 inches long would be needed. It has been computed that for Mark 19 feet would be required, for Matthew 30 feet, and for Luke 31 or 32 feet, and for John 23 feet 6 inches. It is manifest that in the earliest times each of the longer writings would be circulated in a separate roll, and that no complete copy of the New Testament, or of the four Gospels, can have been made. Textual critics have pointed out the consequent difficulty of verifying references, with the result that quotations were frequently made from memory. To handle a book like a modern roll of wall paper cannot have been easy, and one can see that some better method of production would be sure of an early welcome.

The Codex Form. A papyrus codex was formed by folding a number of sheets so as to produce a quire after the manner of a modern book. It was long supposed that the codex did not come into existence until early in the fourth century when the vellum codex, as seen in Codex Vaticanus and Codex Sinaiticus, was produced, but recent discoveries, of which the Chester Beatty Papyri and a small fragment of John's Gospel (P[52]) are examples, prove that the codex form was used for the New Testament writings in the first half of the second and in the third centuries. Rolls continued to be used, especially for pagan books, but the popularity of the Christian writings and the need to consult them frequently fostered the use of the codex form.

The Character of the Writing. Writing in papyrus MSS was produced in columns, usually two or three inches wide and frequently leaning a little to the right. Two styles of writing were adopted, a literary and a non-literary hand. In the literary hand the characters are for the most part separate one from another. Ligatures are rare and the characters are smaller than those found in the later vellum MSS. Neatly and carefully written by professional scribes, manuscripts produced in this style are the classical writings and important documents. The non-literary hand was that of every-day use. Often dated, they were written with the utmost freedom. The writing was cursive, that is to say, the letters were generally connected one with another. About the eighth century a literary cursive came into existence, and this prepared the way for MSS of the later minuscule period.

In papyrus MSS corrections were made between the lines or in the margins at the top or bottom. Accents, breathings, and other punctuation marks are found to some extent in the literary papyri in longer words, or in shorter words which might otherwise cause difficulty, but in the non-literary papyri they are almost non-existent. Pauses were marked by small blank spaces in the text or by a dot above or in the line. The beginning of a paragraph was indicated by a short line below the beginning of the line in which the pause occurs. There were no capital letters at the beginning of a clause and no unfinished lines.

The Importance of the Papyrus Period. Several characteristics of the early papyrus MSS need to be remembered in order to appreciate their textual importance. First, the New Testament writings were neither written nor copied as literary works. Many copies indeed must have been written by private persons of varying degrees of literary skill. Secondly, it must be borne in mind that during times of persecution it would be the better copies, preserved by the great churches, which would be most likely to be destroyed. For these two reasons it is easy to see that great differences of reading would inevitably arise. Thirdly, as the New Testament books were not yet regarded as sacred writings, glosses and marginal comments would sometimes come to be inserted into the text itself. Finally, papyrus material is very perishable. Most of the papyrus MSS which have

survived consist of broken fragments, with the result that
restored readings are conjectural. These facts have greatly
influenced the textual history of the New Testament in
general. F. G. Kenyon has said, 'It is to its fortunes during
the papyrus period that the New Testament owes its peculiar
textual history.'[1] Subsequent discoveries have amply
confirmed this judgement.

From the facts observed above it must not be supposed
that the text of the New Testament as we have it to-day is
untrustworthy. In the opinion of many textual critics there
is good reason to think that the great vellum MSS of the
Uncial Period were for the most part carefully executed and
rest upon good papyrus MSS. Moreover, as already pointed
out, the abundance of our textual material means that, with
a large measure of certainty, the genuine text can be
obtained by the use of scientific principles and methods.

The Principal Papyrus Manuscripts.

P[1] This and the next two MSS were discovered at
Oxyrhynchus and published by Grenfell and Hunt. Its
date is the third or fourth century. It contains parts of
Mt. i and is now at Philadelphia. The text is of the β type.

P[5] This MS contains Jn. i. 23–31, 33–41, xvi. 14–30,
xx. 11–17, 19–25. Its date is the third century and its text
of the β type.

P[13] Contains Heb. ii. 14–v. 5, x. 8–22, 29–xi. 13, xi.
28–xii. 17. Its date is the late third or fourth century.
It is especially important because it contains parts of
Hebrews which are wanting in B.

P[38] Ac. xviii. 27–xix. 6, xix. 12–16. The third or fourth
century. It often agrees with D and is of the δ type.

P[45] This and the two following MSS are known as the
Chester Beatty Papyri. Along with nine other MSS (eight of
the Old Testament and one of the Book of Enoch) they
were acquired from dealers in Egypt by Mr. A. Chester

---

[1] *Handbook to the Textual Criticism of the New Testament* (1901), 31.

Beatty in 1931.[1] P[45] contains portions of all four Gospels and the Acts.[2] Its date is the third century and the text is Caesarean, with readings from other families. The format is the Codex form (see above).

P[46] Contains portions of the Pauline Epistles (from Rom.–I Thess.) and of Heb. The third century.

P[47] Part of the Apocalypse. Late third century.

P[52] (Pap. Ryl. 457). This valuable MS was discovered by C. H. Roberts[3] among papyri acquired by Hunt in 1920. It contains Jn. xviii. 31–3, 37f. It is the earliest fragment of any New Testament MS we now possess and belongs to the first half of the second century. It proves that the Gospel of John was in circulation in Egypt at this early date.

P[66] (Pap. Bodmer II).[4] This MS contains Jn. i. i–vi. 11, vi. 35–xiv. 26, and fragments of Jn. xv.–xxi. Its date is *c.* A.D. 200 and it is in the Codex form.

P[75] (Pap. Bodmer xiv–xv) contains Lk. viii. 10–17, Jn. i–iv, viii–ix, and other fragments. A Codex, it is provisionally dated A.D. 175–225. It often agrees with the B text.[5]

Other Recent Discoveries. These bear upon the background of the Gospels. They include the following:

P Egerton 2. This MS was purchased in the summer of 1934 from a dealer and was obtained by the Trustees of the British Museum. It consists of fragments from an otherwise unknown Gospel which have been edited by H. I. Bell and T. C. Skeat.[6] The fragments record a dispute between

---

[1] Announced in *The Times*, 19th Nov. 1931.

[2] Cf. R. V. G. Tasker, *JTS*, xxviii, 383–93. For a fuller account of the Chester Beatty Papyri see F. G. Kenyon, *Recent Developments*, 51–63, 97–8.

[3] Cf. *An Unpublished Fragment of the Fourth Gospel* (1935).

[4] Cf. Victor Martin, 'Papyrus Bodmer II, Évangile de Jean chap. 1–14,' in *Bibliotheca Bodmeriana*, v (1956); A. F. J. Klijn *NTS*, iii, 327–34; C. K. Barrett, *ET*, lxviii, 174–7.

[5] Cf. B. M. Metzger, *ET*, lxxiii. 201–3.

[6] Cf. H. I. Bell and T. C. Skeat, *Fragments of an Unknown Gospel* (1935).

Jesus and the lawyers (cf. Jn. v. 29, 45, ix. 29), the healing of a leper (cf. Mk. i. 40–5), the question about tribute (cf. Mk. xii. 13–17, Lk. vi. 46), and a miracle by the Jordan which tells how Jesus sprinkled water which sends forth fruit. The fragments are dated by experts *c.* A.D. 150 and the MS is said to have been written by a practised writer, but not a professional scribe. There are no accents or breathings and little punctuation. The MS is not a collection of sayings or a Gospel harmony, but is part of a real Gospel not connected with any known apocryphal Gospel. The tradition it contains is quite independent of the Synoptic Gospels and is either based on John or was itself used by John or comes from a source also used by John.

The Dura Fragment. This vellum fragment is part of a Greek version of Tatian's *Diatessaron* (see later) discovered at Dura on the Euphrates among the ruins of a Roman fort.[1] It consists of fourteen lines from the Synoptic Gospels which describe the request of Joseph of Arimathaea for the body of Jesus. It is dated *c.* A.D. 225 and is of great interest since otherwise the *Diatessaron* is known to us only in Syriac and Latin. Whether Tatian's Gospel harmony was first written in Greek or Syriac is a disputed question which the Dura Fragment appeared to settle. Unfortunately, its text contains two readings which appear to be mistranslations of the Syriac.[2] If so the question is still open.[3]

The Dead Sea Scrolls. These MSS have been discovered from 1947 onwards in the Qumran region near the Dead Sea.[4] They illustrate Jewish religious ideas some of which are comparable to those found in the Fourth Gospel and are variously dated in the centuries immediately before and after the time of Christ. The Qumran sect, the ruins of whose

[1] Cf. Kenyon, *The Text of the Greek Bible*, 115f.
[2] Cf. C. K. Barrett, *LQHR*, Apr. 1958, 121.
[3] See further C. H. Kraeling, *Studies and Documents*, III (1935).
[4] Cf. T. H. Gaster, *The Scriptures of the Dead Sea Sect* (1957); Millar Burrows, *The Dead Sea Scrolls* (1956); H. H. Rowley, *The Dead Sea Scrolls and the New Testament* (1957).

monastic buildings have been uncovered, is variously assigned to Pharisees, Sadducees, Essenes, and Zealots, and by some scholars their lustrations and emphasis upon Baptism are identified with the teaching and practice of John the Baptist. Besides recording the rules of the community, the scrolls consist of commentaries on Old Testament books, including Isaiah and Habakkuk. They contribute nothing to textual questions relating to the New Testament, but raise interesting questions regarding its teaching. A 'Teacher of Righteousness' is mentioned in the scrolls, but his identity, if he was a real person, is not known.[1]

The Gospel of Truth. This writing is an ancient Gnostic text contained in what is known as the Jung Codex.[2] Its teaching is said to be a kind of Christian Gnosticism Valentinian in character. Apart from the light it throws upon some aspects of second-century Christianity it is of value for its testimony to the canonicity of many New Testament books during this period.

The Gospel of Thomas. Like the Gospel of Truth this document has no direct bearing on textual criticism, but it may be mentioned here because its discovery has attracted considerable attention since 1956. It is not a Gospel at all but a collection of some 114 sayings attributed to Jesus and alleged to be written by the Apostle Thomas. Its importance is that it contains a very old Gospel tradition not directly taken from our canonical Gospels but derived from another source.[3]

From the above it will be seen how interesting and important recent discoveries are, and the hope is encouraged that both for textual and doctrinal purposes further finds may await us.

[1] Cf. Barrett, *LQHR*, 120.   [2] Cf. Barrett, *ET*, lxix, 167–70.
[3] Cf. R. McL. Wilson, *NTS*, 5, 273–6, G. Quispel, *NTS*, 5, 276–90. Whether, however, it implies the existence of the Synoptic sayings-tradition and recasts it, is a question for consideration. Cf. H.-W. Bartsch, *NTS*, 6, 249–61.

IV

THE UNCIAL PERIOD

THE uncial MSS were written on vellum from the fourth to the ninth or tenth centuries in large capital Greek letters. The name is derived from a phrase of Jerome in his Preface to the Book of Job. Jerome complains that in his day many books were written *uncialibus, ut aiunt, litteris,* 'in inch-long letters, one may say', an exaggerated description of the characters used. Eight of the most important uncials are described below and a few others later.

ℵ, *Codex Sinaiticus.* This handsome MS was discovered by the great textual critic Constantin Tischendorf at the monastery of St. Catherine on Mount Sinai in 1844. The fascinating story of the manner in which he ultimately obtained possession of it in 1859 is described by Kenyon[1] and others. It was presented to the Czar of Russia, Alexander II, and lodged at St. Petersburg, but was purchased for the British nation for £100,000 and after conditioning was placed in the British Museum.[2] It now contains a few parts of the Old Testament, all the New Testament, and, in addition, the Epistle of Barnabas and in part the Shepherd of Hermas. There are four columns to the page. Later correctors of the MS have been distinguished by Tischendorf: in the fourth century ℵᵃ, in the sixth ℵᵇ, and in the seventh ℵᶜ ᵒʳ ᶜᵃ, ℵᶜᵇ, and ℵᶜᶜ, but it is now usual to use the symbol ℵᶜ which indicates the reading of a corrector. Its date is the fourth

---

[1] *Handbook to the Textual Criticism of the New Testament,* 48–50.

[2] An account was given by T. C. Skeat in the *Daily Telegraph and Morning Post,* 12th Jan. 1938, 'Clues and Blemishes in the Codex Sinaiticus.'

century. Like Codex Vaticanus (B) it was probably produced in Egypt and in the seventh century was at Caesarea. Its text is of the β type, but contains some δ readings.

B, *Codex Vaticanus*. This important MS has been in the Vatican Library at Rome since 1481, where it still remains. It was difficult of access until 1868, but since then has been repeatedly examined. Originally it contained the whole Greek Bible, but now the New Testament lacks Hebrews from ix. 14 onwards, the Pastoral Epistles, Philemon, and the Apocalypse. B has three columns to the page and, like ℵ, was probably produced in Egypt in the fourth century at the command of the Emperor Constantine. It is the chief authority for the β text.

A, *Codex Alexandrinus*. The original home of this MS was Alexandria. It is now preserved in the British Museum. It contains nearly all the New Testament, but originally the whole Greek Bible. In it the Epistle of Clement of Rome follows immediately upon the Apocalypse without a break. The date of compilation is the fifth century. The text is mixed. In the Gospels it is of the α type, but in the Acts, the Epistles, and the Apocalypse it is of the β type, and so is of greater value.

C, *Codex Ephraemi*. This MS is a palimpsest, that is, a MS in which the original writing has been rubbed down and a second work superimposed, in this case thirty-eight sermons of Ephraem of Syria. Hence its name. Originally it contained the whole Greek Bible. In consequence of its fortunes C is sadly mutilated, but parts of all the New Testament books, except 2 Thessalonians and 2 John, can be read with difficulty. It is a fifth-century MS and its text is mixed. In the Gospels it often supports the β text. Brought to France by Catherine Medici it is now preserved in the Bibliothèque Nationale in Paris. Recently its text has been examined, with important results, by Dr. R. W. Lyon of Princeton University, U.S.A.[1]

[1] *NTS*, 5, 260–72.

D, Codex Bezae. This interesting and valuable MS was obtained by the Reformer Theodore Beza from the monastery of St. Irenaeus at Lyons and presented by him to the University of Cambridge in 1581. It contains, with gaps, the Gospels, the Acts, and part of 3 John, the Gospels being arranged in the Western order (Mt., Jn., Lk., Mk.). There is one column to the page. The Gospels are transcribed in Greek on the left side and in Latin on the right. Corresponding to the symbol D, which describes the Greek text, the sign 'd' represents the Latin text. D was formerly assigned to the sixth century, but F. C. Burkitt argued for the fifth century and Kenyon regards this date as probable. South France, South Italy, Sicily, and Sardinia have been suggested as its place of origin. Codex Bezae is the chief authority for the δ text; it often agrees with the Old Latin Version. It is characterized by a series of remarkable omissions in Luke, especially in chapters xxii and xxiv, and by many striking additions and variations in the Acts.

W, The Freer Manuscript. Or the Washington Codex I. This MS was acquired by Mr. C. L. Freer of Detroit and edited by Professor H. A. Sanders of Michigan.[1] It is preserved at Washington. The MS contains the four Gospels in the Western order and a second MS (Washington Codex II) contains portions of the Pauline Epistles. The text of W is mixed. It is especially valuable in Mark, for, while Mk. i–v. 30 has a δ text, the text of Mk. v. 31–xvi. 8 is in Streeter's view,[2] Caesarean. Probably of Western origin, W appears to have been carried at some period to Caesarea. Its date is the fifth century. An interesting feature is an alternative ending or addition to Mark inserted after verse 14 in xvi. 9–20.[3]

L, Codex Regius. This MS is in the Bibliothèque Nationale

[1] Mr. Freer acquired four MSS, two containing Deuteronomy, Joshua, and a Psalter, and two New Testament MSS as described above.   [2] *The Four Gospels,* 600.

[3] For the text of this ending see the Note on Mk. xvi. 9–20 on p. 89f.

in Paris. Its date is the eighth century. It contains the 'Shorter Ending' of Mark as well as the 'Longer Ending', xvi. 9–20. The text is of the β type.

Θ, *Codex Koridethi.* This MS was discovered in a remote valley in the Caucasus 'where', says Streeter,[1] 'it had long been a kind of village fetish'. Earlier it belonged to a monastery at Koridethi at the eastern end of the Black Sea. It has been available for study since 1913 at Tiflis. Its date is the eighth century.[2] Its text is mixed, but according to Streeter and Lake it is the chief authority for the eastern text. Its principal allies are the minuscule MSS fam.1, fam. 13, 28, 565, and 700. A notable reading in it is 'Jesus Barabbas' in Mt. xxvii. 16f.[3]

The above are the most valuable uncial MSS. There are many other uncials, some of which are mentioned below, but most of these contain the later Byzantine text (the α text) which is the basis of the Textus Receptus used in the Authorized Version. It should be remembered that some of the better cursive MSS are quite as valuable as A, C, and W, and more valuable than any uncial after the eight described above. This fact illustrates the statement of Streeter,[4] 'The precedence of MSS depends, not on their age, but on their pedigree.'

A few additional MSS may be mentioned which have points of special interest and significance. They are:

Δ, *Codex Sangallensis.* A Graeco-Latin MS of the Gospels with a β text in Mark.

N, *Codex Purpureus Petropolitanus.* Forms a group with Codices Σ (Rossanensis), O (Sinopensis), and Φ (Beratinus). While mainly of the α type, these MSS contain Caesarean readings.[5]

P_2, *Codex Porphyrianus.* Contains parts of Acts, the Epistles, and the Apocalypse. It is one of the few MSS containing the Apocalypse.

---

[1] *Op. cit.,* 79.   [2] Or the ninth century   [3] See later, p. 81f.
[4] *Op. cit.,* 50.   [5] Cf. Streeter, *op. cit.,* 575–7.

Ξ *Codex Zacynthius.* In the Library of the British and Foreign Bible Society. Its text is akin to that of B, and it has the same section-divisions, which are found also in 579.

Ψ, *Codex Laurensis.* With L this MS has both the 'Shorter' and 'Longer' endings in Mark.

D_2, *Codex Claromontanus.* Forms a group with F_2 (Augiensis), and G_3 (Boernerianus), which have a δ text in the Pauline Epistles.[1]

H_3, *Codex Coislinianus.* Has an eastern text in the Pauline Epistles.

The numbers attached to these MSS are used to distinguish them from Gospel MSS named with the same letters and are not commonly used in readings where the identity of the writing in question is clear.

Some Notable Readings in Codex Bezae (D). D has a number of additions and omissions to a remarkable degree, especially in Luke and the Acts. In these cases it frequently has the support of the Old Latin Version. The list which follows is only a selection, but it has the advantage of illustrating the many problems which the textual critic has to face. After Lk. vi. 4 D inserts a short narrative which may well be authentic, 'On the same day he saw a man working on the Sabbath and he said unto him, "Man, if you know what you are doing, blessed are you; but if you do not know, you are accursed and a transgressor of the law." '
In Lk. ix. 55 it reads, 'And he said, "You know not of what spirit you are," ' and it has a fuller account of the Lord's Prayer in Lk. xi. 2–4.

But the more interesting and important features are the *omissions* of D in Luke. So prone is this MS to *add* that Westcott and Hort,[2] in spite of their low estimate of the value of the 'Western Text' (see above, ch. II) regard the omissions

---

[1] Codex Sangermanensis (E_3) is a copy of D_2.

[2] Westcott and Hort, *The NT in Greek*, 295, distinguish between 'Western omissions' and 'Western non-interpolations', a term they apply to Mt. xxvii. 49, Lk. xxii. 19b–20, xxiv. 3, 6, 12, 36, 40, 51, 52 using double brackets for these passages ('the Lord Jesus' in xxiv. 3).

of D as preserving the original text, and they speak of them as 'Western non-interpolations'. To-day in many quarters there is a marked tendency to accept many of the passages omitted by D, especially Lk. xxii, 19*b*–20, the longer text in the Lucan account of the Supper.[1] From the omissions in question the following may be mentioned. The most important are in Lk. xxii and xxiv.

Lk. v. 39: 'And no man having drunk old wine desireth new: for he says, "The old is good" '.

Lk. vii. 7*a*: 'Wherefore neither thought I myself worthy to come unto thee'.

Lk. x. 41f: 'concerning many things. But few things are needful, or one'.

Lk. xi. 35f: 'Look therefore whether the light that is in thee be not darkness. If therefore thy whole body be full of light, having no part dark, it shall be wholly full of light, as when the lamp with its bright shining gives thee light'.

Lk. xii. 19: 'laid up for many years; take your ease, eat, drink'.

Lk. xix. 25: 'And they said unto him, " Lord, he has ten pounds" '.

Lk. xxii. 19*b*–20: ' "which is given for you: this do in remembrance of me". And the cup in like manner after supper, saying, "This cup is the new covenant in my blood, even that which is poured out for you" '.

Lk. xxiv. 6: ' "He is not here, but is risen" '.

Lk. xxiv. 12: 'But Peter arose, and ran unto the tomb; and stooping and looking in, he sees the linen cloths by themselves; and he departed to his home, wondering at that which was come to pass'.

Lk. xxiv. 36: 'and he says to them, "Peace be unto you" '.

Lk. xxiv. 40: 'And when he had said this, he showed them his hands and his feet'.

Lk. xxiv. 51: 'and was carried up into heaven'.

Lk. xxiv. 52: 'worshipping him'.

[1] Cf. J. Jeremias, *The Eucharistic Words of Jesus*, 87–106.

The D readings in the Acts are *additions* and variations either made by the editor of the δ text or excised by the editor of the β text. Reviving an older explanation Blass maintained that Luke issued the Gospel and the Acts in two editions, but this hypothesis has not been widely adopted. The additions are numerous and can be seen in J. M. Wilson's *The Acts of the Apostles from Codex Bezae* (1923) printed in a translation of the MS in thick type. All that can be given here is a representative selection.

Ac. v. 15: 'For they were set free from every sickness which each one of them had'.

Ac. v. 39: 'neither you nor kings nor tyrants: keep away therefore from these men'.

Ac. viii. 24: 'And he (Simon) ceased not to shed many tears'.

Ac. x. 25: 'And as Peter was drawing near to Caesarea one of the servants ran forward and announced that he was come. And Cornelius sprang up and (met him)'.

Ac. xi. 2: '(Peter) therefore for a considerable time wished to journey to Jerusalem; and he called to him the brethren, and stablished them; making a long speech, and teaching them throughout the villages: he also went to meet them, and he reported to them the grace of (God)'.

Ac. xi. 28: 'And there was much rejoicing; and when we were gathered together'. (An additional 'We' passage.)

Ac. xii. 10: 'and went down the seven steps'.

Ac. xii. 23: 'And he came down from the throne, and while he was still living (he was eaten of worms)'.

Ac. xiii. 29: 'they asked Pilate to crucify him. (And) when they had obtained this also'.

Ac. xiv. 7: 'And the whole multitude was moved at the teaching'.

Ac. xv. 2: 'for Paul spoke strongly maintaining that they should remain so as when they believed; but those who had come down from Jerusalem'.

Ac. xv. 20 (and 29): 'and that whatsoever they would not should be done to them you do not to others'.

c

Ac. xvi. 35: '(the magistrates) assembled together into the market place, and recollecting the earthquake that had happened (they sent)'.

Ac. xvii. 15: 'But he passed by Thessaly for he was forbidden to proclaim the word to them'.

Ac. xviii. 27: 'Now certain Corinthians were sojourning in Ephesus, and having heard him (Apollos), they exhorted him to cross with them into their own country; and when he consented the Ephesians wrote to the disciples in Corinth that they should receive the man. (And) when he sojourned in Achaia . . .'.

Ac. xix. 1: 'when Paul, according to his private wish, desired to go to Jerusalem, the Spirit told him to return into Asia'.

Ac. xix. 9: '(in the school of) one (Tyrannus) from the fifth till the tenth hour'.

Ac. xxi. 16: '(And) when they came to a certain village, we stayed with (Mnason, a certain Cyprian, an old disciple)'.

These and other readings of the kind should be studied in the light of the evidence as a whole.[1] Besides the Old Latin and the Old Syriac they are often supported by later citations. Religious in tendency, harmonistic, and explanatory, they appear in some cases to rest on early tradition. They illustrate the freedom with which the text of Lk./Ac. was treated in the first half of the second century. It should be remembered, however, that the additions and omissions of D present a special problem and are much more numerous than in the early MSS as a whole.

[1] Cf. F. G. Kenyon, *The Text of the Greek Bible*, 213–38; C. S. C, Williams, *Alterations to the Text of the Synoptic Gospels and Acts* (1951), 54–82. See also J. H. Ropes, *The Beginnings of Christianity*, vol. III (1926), ccxxviii, and A. C. Clark, *Acts of the Apostles* (1933).

V

THE MINUSCULE MANUSCRIPTS

FROM the ninth century onwards MSS were written on vellum in the minuscule hand in response to the need for books more convenient to handle. Uncials were too bulky and took too long to produce. Accordingly, as already explained, a literary cursive came to be used by scribes in the production of MSS. Like the uncials these MSS were written upon vellum and in the codex form. Over 2,400 of them exist of which about 1,000 contain the Gospels or some part of them. The great majority contain the α text, but a few, evidently copies from good uncials no longer in existence, contain earlier texts, β, δ, and eastern, and are therefore valuable for purposes of textual criticism. Some of them belong to families or groups ultimately derived from a common archetype. Several of the most important minuscule MSS are described below.

Fam. 1 (or f. 1). This group consists of 1, 118, 131, and 209, which were shown to constitute a family by Kirsopp Lake.[1] For this reason the group is sometimes designated by the symbol λ. Codex 1 is of interest because it is one of the MSS used by Erasmus in preparing the first printed Greek Testament. It is now at Basle. These MSS belong to the eleventh and twelfth centuries and contain a Caesarean text together with readings of other types. Other MSS belonging to the same family are 22, 872 (in Mk.), 1278, and 1582.

Fam. 13 (or f. 13). Or the 'Ferrar Group', otherwise known as φ. The minuscules 13, 69, 124, and 346 were shown to be a family by Dr. W. H. Ferrar of Dublin. Other

---

[1] *Cambridge Texts and Studies*, vii, 3 (1902).

MSS have subsequently been added to the family as the result of further research, including 230, 543, 788, 826, 828, 983, 1689, and 1709. The original four are preserved at Paris, Leicester, Vienna, and Milan respectively. 13, 124, and 346 were written at Calabria in the twelfth century and 69 in the fifteenth from MSS dependent on an archetype probably brought from the east. The text is mainly of the α type, but often contains Caesarean readings. The story of the woman taken in adultery (the *pericope adulterae*) is transferred to follow Lk. xxi. 38.

28. This MS of the eleventh or twelfth century is also at Paris and contains the Gospels. It has a Caesarean text, but contains δ readings.

33. Eichhorn called this MS 'the queen of the cursives'. It is at Paris and is a ninth-century MS. The text is of the β type. It strongly supports B.

81. Written in A.D. 1044 this MS contains the Acts only 'for which it is the best of the minuscules, ranking with the leading uncials in quality'.[1] In the older commentaries it is described as Act. 61. Preserved at the British Museum it contains parts of Ac. i–iv, vii–xvii, and xxiii. Its text is of the β type.

565. This handsome MS written with gold letters on purple vellum is known as 'the Empress Theodora's Codex'. It is a ninth-century MS and is at Leningrad. It is a most important ally of Θ in Mark.

579. Thirteenth century, at Paris. It contains the double ending in Mark. It has an α text in Matthew, and a β text in Mark, Luke, and John, and is said to be derived from a sixth century uncial. 'The value of a MS of this kind appears where it supports a reading of B, ℵ, or L, which otherwise is unsupported.'[2]

700. 700 is at the British Museum and is a twelfth-century MS. It has a β text along with Caesarean readings.

---

[1] F. G. Kenyon, *The Text of the Greek Bible*, 106.
[2] Cf. Streeter, *op. cit.*, 63.

In Lk. xi. 2 it reads, 'Let thy Holy Spirit come upon us and cleanse us,' and in this reading has the support of 162. Streeter maintains that the probability is high that this is what Luke wrote.[1]

The Lectionaries. During the minuscule period many Lectionaries consisting of passages or lections for use in church services came into existence. More than 1,600 MSS of the kind are known. The lectionary has been described as 'the pulpit Bible of the Middle Ages'. The lections chosen range from two or three verses to three or four chapters, but usually consist of about ten verses. A collection from the Gospels was known as an Evangeliarium and one from the Acts as an Apostolos. Two kinds are distinguished, the Synaxarion consisting of lections for the ecclesiastical year from Easter to Easter and the Menologion containing lections for the calendar year from September to August. Until recent times the Lectionaries have been generally ignored because for the most part they contain the late ecclesiastical text, but E. C. Colwell has insisted that in the Gospels they agree in the text to a remarkable degree which suggests that there is a definite lectionary text existing from the eighth to the sixteenth century. This becomes apparent if we study them lection by lection and not simply as separate MSS. Early readings are often embedded in them. D. W. Riddle, who with E. C. Colwell has made a careful study of the lectionaries,[2] points out that the lections from Mark (amounting to three-fourths of the Gospel) contain 347 variants from the Received Text. Of these variants 200 have the support of ℵ, 185 of B, 163 of C, 191 of L, and 202 are in the text of Westcott and Hort, while only 27 have the support of D and its allies. On the other side features characteristic of the lectionaries have to be allowed for; introductory phrases like 'The Lord said', additional words at the end of the

---

[1] *Op. cit.*, 277.
[2] Cf. E. C. Colwell and D. W. Riddle, *Prolegomena to the Study of the Lectionary Text of the Gospels*, i. (1933), 38f.

lections, and insertions from other narratives. Colwell suggests that the presence of the *pericope adulterae* after Lk. xxi. 38 in fam. 13 is due to lectionary influence.[1] The lectionaries contribute to our knowledge of the history of the text and, since they are conservative in tendency, they supply important evidence for the text itself. They are being increasingly quoted in critical texts and are indicated by the letter 'l' (e.g. l 48 &c.).

[1] *Op. cit.*, 19.

VI

THE VERSIONS

FROM the second century onwards the New Testament books were translated into other languages for the use of Christians who did not normally speak Greek or did not employ it as a first language in everyday life. The three principal versions are (1) the Latin (the Old Latin and the Vulgate), (2) the Syriac, from which the Armenian and Georgian were derived, and (3) the Coptic or Egyptian. Other versions of less importance are the Ethiopic, the Arabic, and the Gothic.

The Use and Importance of the Versions. The principal versions are of the greatest textual importance because they were made at an early date from Greek MSS no longer extant. Thus they bear indirect witness to early types of text. It is generally allowed that for the most part they appear to represent a faithful translation of the underlying Greek. In using the versions it is necessary to know as far as possible (1) the true text of the version in question since these like the Greek MSS were exposed to scribal corruption, (2) whether or not the version is a translation from the Greek, (3) the date of the translation, and (4) its relation to other authorities for the New Testament text.

I. THE LATIN VERSIONS

THE OLD LATIN VERSION. Its place of origin was probably North Africa and later Rome and Gaul. At first a Latin version would not be required in the Church at Rome, for in many respects this was a Greek speaking Church. This fact is illustrated by the existence of St. Paul's Epistle

to the Romans written in Greek. On the other hand Greek
would be little known in North Africa where Christianity
was preached at a comparatively early date. The period
of the first translations cannot be definitely fixed, but was
probably the middle of the second century. We possess a
considerable number of Old Latin MSS which are classified
as the African and the European MSS.

The African Latin. The more primitive form of the version.
Its best representatives are *Codex Bobiensis* (k) of the fourth
or fifth century and *Codex Palatinus* (e) of the fifth century.
Its text is supported by the quotations of Cyprian, Bishop
of Carthage A.D. 248–58.

The European Latin. Its best representatives are *Codex
Vercellensis* (a) of the fourth century and *Codex Veronensis*
(b) of the fifth century, supported by the quotations of
Irenaeus, Bishop of Lyons until *c.* 202.

A third type, *the Italian,* used to be distinguished from the
above, represented by *Codex Brixianus* (f) of the sixth century *and Codex Monacensis* (q) of the seventh, but it is now
regarded as a fourth-century revision of the European Latin.

The Text. Belongs to the δ type. It often agrees with D,
for example in the addition in Mt. xx. 28, the omissions of
Lk. xxiv, and many of the additions in the Acts. This is
especially true of the African Latin.

THE VULGATE. The Vulgate is not an independent version,
but a revision made by Jerome in 383–6 at the command of
Pope Damasus from Old Latin MSS corrected by Greek
MSS. Jerome's principles and methods are explained in his
Preface to the Gospels (383). Alterations were made only
in important passages. Smaller mistakes were left uncor-
rected so as not to disturb the familiar language. In the later
New Testament books which followed, his revision was more
perfunctory. His rendering of the Old Testament was a
new translation from the Hebrew.

Later History. In the course of time corruptions crept into the Vulgate text. It was revised by Alcuin *c.* 800 and by others. It was first printed in 1456 in the Mazarin Bible and in the Complutensian Polyglot[1] in 1522. In accordance with a decree of the Council of Trent (8th April, 1546) an official edition was published at the command of Pope Sixtus V in 1590, but in 1592 after the death of Sixtus the so-called Clementine edition was issued by the command of Clement VIII, and this is the official Latin Bible text of the Roman Catholic Church to the present day. Bishop Wordsworth and H. J. White produced a critical edition of the New Testament which was finished by others in 1954. Pius X commissioned the Benedictine Order in 1907 to prepare an edition and it is in course of production in Rome.[2]

The MSS of the Vulgate. The best MSS belong to the Northumbrian group produced at Wearmouth and Jarrow under the direction of Ceolfrid. Some of the most important are:

Codex Amiatinus (A, am). This is the best MS. Now in the Laurentian Library at Florence. It was written early in the eighth century.

Codex Lindisfarnensis (Y). It was written in honour of St. Cuthbert who died A.D. 687. Its text is akin to that of A. In the British Museum.

Codex Fuldensis (F, fu). Written at Fulda in Germany at the order of Victor Bishop of Capua (541–6). The Gospels are arranged in the form of a harmony which follows the arrangement of Tatian's *Diatessaron.*

Codex Cavensis (C). At La Cava in South Italy C is of the ninth century and is the chief representative of the Spanish family of MSS.

Codex Dublinensis (D), or the *Book of Armagh.* It represents the Irish type of text. It is at Dublin and is of the eighth or ninth century.

---

[1] Contains the OT in three columns in Hebrew, Latin, and Greek and the NT in two columns in Greek and Latin. Produced at Alcala (Complutum).

[2] Cf. A. Wikenhauser, *New Testament Introduction,* 105f.

Codex Kenanensis (Q), or the *Book of Kells*. Eighth century. Beautifully illuminated. It also is at Dublin in the Library of Trinity College and represents the Irish type of text.

The Greek MSS used by Jerome. On the whole Jerome appears to have used MSS like ℵ, B, and L, but sometimes he used MSS unlike any we now possess.

2. THE SYRIAC VERSIONS

These include: Tatian's *Diatessaron* (sy^d), the Old Syriac (the Sinaitic (sy^s) and the Curetonian (sy^c)), the Peshitta (sy^p), the Philoxenian (sy^{ph}), the Harklean (sy^h), and the Palestinian (or Jerusalem) Syriac (sy^{pal}).

THE DIATESSARON (sy^d). From Eusebius and others we know that about A.D. 170–80 Tatian composed a harmony of the Four Gospels. The original work is now lost but from various sources much of its text can be reconstructed. The sources are (1) an Armenian version of a commentary or series of homilies on the *Diatessaron* by Ephraem Syrus (d. 373), (2) quotations in the homilies of Aphraates (337–45), (3) two copies of an Arabic translation, (4) Codex Fuldensis, (5) mediaeval Dutch and Old Italian harmonies and a Persian translation.

Original Language. Opinion is still divided on the question whether the *Diatessaron* was first composed in Greek or in Syriac. Earlier opinion favoured the former, but much recent opinion supports the latter.[1] The Dura Fragment (see earlier, p. 13) would settle the question in favour of Greek, were it not for the doubt whether the fragment belongs to a Greek translation from the Syriac for the use of the Greek settlers in Dura-Europus.

The Text. The text is of the δ type with many β readings.

[1] Among modern scholars who think that the *Diatessaron* was written in Syriac, Wikenhauser names D. Plooij (1923), A Baumstark (1931), C. Peters (1939), P. Kahle (1947) and A. Vööbus (1948), cf. *New Testament Introduction*, 113.

THE OLD SYRIAC.[1] The Old Syriac is represented by two
MSS only, the Sinaitic and the Curetonian, of which the
Sinaitic is the older.

The Sinaitic (sy[s]) is a fourth-century MS discovered by two
sisters, Mrs. Lewis and Mrs. Gibson, in the monastery of
St. Catherine at Mount Sinai in 1892 and published by them
in 1894. It is a palimpsest and contains considerable
portions of the four Gospels.

The Curetonian Syriac (sy[c]) is a fifth-century MS acquired
in 1842 by Archdeacon Tattam and others from the monastery of St. Mary Deipara in the Nitrian desert in Egypt and
identified by W. Cureton of the British Museum as containing a hitherto unknown version of the Gospels. It was
published in 1858.

The Text of the Old Syriac. The text is of the δ type; it
often agrees with D and the Old Latin. F. C. Burkitt[2]
maintained that the underlying Greek text was derived from
the older text at Antioch, and Streeter[3] takes the same view.
The textual relationship between the *Diatessaron* and the
Old Syriac is a much disputed question. In view of important differences between the two Kenyon[4] maintains that the
Diatessaron was not made from the Old Syriac. The only
thing that is certain, Black[5] observes, is that a connexion
did exist between the two.

The Date of the Old Syriac. Kenyon[6] thinks it probable
that the Old Syriac version was made after the *Diatessaron*
about A.D. 200. Black[7] suggests the second half of the second
century and thinks that the earliest Syriac Gospel translations drew on the apocryphal Gospels.

Notable Readings of the Old Syriac Version. Like D the

---

[1] For the *Diatessaron* and the Old Syriac see F. C. Burkitt, *Evangelion da-Mepharreshe*; M. Black, *An Aramaic Approach to the Gospels
and Acts*, 2nd ed. (1954), 197–205.

[2] *Evangelion da-Mepharreshe*, ii, 254.   [3] *Op. cit.*, 74f.

[4] *The Text of the Greek Bible*, 121. Kenyon points out that important passages found in the *Diatessaron* are omitted by sy[s] and sy[c].

[5] *Op. cit.*, 199.   [6] *Op. cit.*, 122.   [7] *Op. cit.*, 199, 204.

Old Syriac contains a number of notable readings which have led to much discussion. Among these are the following:

Mt. i. 16. Sy⁸ reads, 'Joseph, to whom was betrothed Mary the Virgin, begat Jesus, who is called Christ,' and syᶜ, 'Joseph, to whom was betrothed Mary the Virgin, who (fem.) bore Jesus Christ'.

Mt. xvi. 2f. Both MSS omit the passage (about signs of weather) with ℵ B fam. 13 (against D).

Mt. xxvii. 16f. Sy⁸ (with Θ fam. 1 and some 'very old' MSS mentioned by Origen) reads 'Jesus Barabbas'.

Mk. xvi. 9–20. Sy⁸ omits this ending, but syᶜ has verses 17–20.

Lk. ix. 55. 'You know not what manner of spirit you are.' Omitted in sy⁸ with ℵ A B C L, but read by syᶜ D (partially) Θ.

Lk. xxii. 17–20 (The Lord's Supper). Sy⁸ has these verses in the order, 19, 20a, 17, 20b, 18; syᶜ 19, 17, 18 (omitting 20), thus avoiding the double reference to the Cup (in most MSS).

Lk. xxii. 43f (The Agony). Sy⁸ omits with ℵ⁴ A B W 13 69 579, but syᶜ retains the verses with ℵ* D Θ etc.

Lk. xxiii. 34, 'Father, forgive them, for they know not what they do'. Sy⁸ omits with ℵ⁴ B D W Θ a b sa¹ bo¹ 579, but syᶜ retains with ℵ* A C e f.

Lk. xxiv. 6, 12, 36, 40, 51, 52. Both sy⁸ and syᶜ have the same omissions as D and the Old Latin.

Jn. xviii. 13–24. Sy⁸ has these verses in the order 13, 24, 14, 15, 19–23, 16–18.

THE PESHITTA (syᵖ). This version, made by Rabbula, Bishop of Edessa A.D. 411–35, became the 'Vulgate' of the Syrian Church. The name means 'simple' or 'single'. It contains both the Old Testament and the New but not 2 Peter, 2 and 3 John, Jude, and the Apocalypse. The four epistles were supplied later from the Philoxenian Version and

¹ For the Sahidic and the Bohairic see p. 34f.

the Apocalypse from the Harklean. About 250 MSS are known to exist, the oldest being of the fifth century.

The older opinion was that the Peshitta was produced in the second or third century, but F. C. Burkitt has shown that the quotations of Ephraem (d. 373) were not taken from this version, but from the *Diatessaron*. The suppression of the *Diatessaron* was the work of Rabbula. The Peshitta belongs to the fifth century.

The text is based on the Old Syriac and later Greek MSS. It is of the α type, but contains a mixture of β and δ readings.

THE PHILOXENIAN (sy^{ph}). The Philoxenian is a revision of the Peshitta in very free and idiomatic Syriac made by a chorepiscopos Polycarp for Philoxenus, the Jacobite or Monophysite Bishop of Mabbog in A.D. 508. It is found in the four minor Catholic Epistles (2 Peter, 2 and 3 John and Jude), now usually printed with the Peshitta, and also the Apocalypse from a twelfth-century MS. The text is of the α type.

THE HARKLEAN SYRIAC (sy^{h}). This version is a revision of the Philoxenian made by Thomas of Harkel in 616 at Alexandria by the aid of MSS of the δ type The rendering is extremely literal. Valuable readings of the same type are added in the margin. They are generally indicated by the sign sy^{h} ^{mg}.

THE PALESTINIAN SYRIAC (sy^{pal}) (sometimes called the Jerusalem Syriac). This version is a lectionary of the Gospels written in a dialect of Western Aramaic, the language 'nearest of all known Christian dialects to that spoken by Jesus and the apostles'.[1] It may have been produced at Antioch, probably in the sixth century. The text is a mixture of the β and δ types. Together with Θ sy^{s} and the Armenian version it reads 'Jesus Barabbas' in Mt. xxvii. 17.

[1] See F. C. Burkitt, *EB*, col. 5005.

3. THE EGYPTIAN (COPTIC) VERSIONS

Coptic is the ancient Egyptian language modified and written in Greek characters. It exists in three dialects: the Bohairic, that of the Bohaira, a district near Alexandria; the Sahidic, spoken in Upper Egypt; and the Middle Egyptian, a group including Fayyumic, Memphitic, and Akhmimic dialects.

At first no version would be required since Greek was in common use. The need would naturally be felt first in Upper Egypt. The earliest version therefore is the Sahidic.[1]

THE SAHIDIC VERSION (sa). This version is represented by many portions of different MSS, and complete MSS of individual books (Acts, John, and the Pauline Epistles) discovered in recent years.[2] The version was probably made in the early part of the third century or the end of the second.[3]

Notable Sahidic Omissions. Kenyon[4] prints an interesting selection of the readings of the Sahidic most of which are omissions shared by ℵ B against D, etc. They are important, not only in themselves, but as illustrating the type of text found in the Sahidic. They include the following, those also omitted by the Bohairic being marked with an asterisk:

Mt. xii. 47.   sa omits with ℵ B (against D W Θ fams. 1 and 13 lat).

* Mt. xviii. 11.   sa omits with ℵ B Θ 1 13 e sy[s] sy[pal] (against D W 28 565 700 lat sy[c] bo).

* Mt. xxiv. 36 ('neither the Son').   sa omits with ℵ[ca] W fam. 1 565 700 vg sy (against ℵ* B D Θ fam. 13 28 it sy[pal]).

---

[1] For the standard work see G. Horner, *The Coptic Versions of the New Testament*, 1898–1924.
[2] Cf. Kenyon, *Recent Developments*, 35–7.
[3] Cf. Kenyon, *The Text of the Greek Bible*, 130.
[4] *The Text of the Greek Bible*, 132f.

* Lk. xxii. 43f (The Agony). sa omits with B bo (against ℵ* D lat sy^c; see further p. 93f).

* Lk. xxiii. 34 ('Father, forgive them . . .'). sa omits with B D bo sy^s (see further p. 94f).

* Jn. v. 4. sa omits with ℵ B D and most Bohairic MSS.

* Jn. vii. 53–viii. 11 (*pericope adulterae*). sa omits with ℵ B W Θ sy^s sy^c bo (against D 28 700, etc.).

The Sahidic agrees with none of the omissions in D and the Old Lat. in Lk. xxiv and has few of the additions of D in the Acts.

The Text. The text is of the β type with an admixture of δ readings. From the above examples it will be seen that in important passages sa agrees with the Alexandrian text represented by ℵ B. The Sahidic is independent of the Bohairic and is derived from different Greek MSS.

THE BOHAIRIC VERSION (bo). This version is represented by many MSS which, although late (the ninth to the twelfth century), contain a substantially pure text. In the care with which they copied MSS the Copts were like the Jews.

The Date. The making of the version is variously dated by scholars from the third to the seventh century.

The Text. The text of the Bohairic is of the β type; is generally agrees with ℵ B. For important features in the text see the list of notable readings omitted by the Sahidic above. The longer ending to Mark (xvi. 9–20) is found in all Bohairic MSS, but two give the shorter ending in the margin.[1]

THE MIDDLE EGYPTIAN VERSIONS. These consist of fragments in more than one translation of which little is known. They are probably independent of the Sahidic and Bohairic and apparently from a different Greek text. Their date is from the fourth to the sixth century. The character of the

---

[1] Cf. F. G. Kenyon, *Handbook*, 158.

text is obscure. 'All that can be said is that the underlying text is substantially the same as that of the Sahidic.'[1]

4. OTHER VERSIONS

THE ARMENIAN VERSION (arm). Whether this version was derived from the Old Syriac[2] or from the Greek[3] is a disputed question. According to early Armenian tradition a version was made by St. Mesrop and St. Sahak (Isaac) about A.D. 400 and later was revised by them after the Council of Ephesus in A.D. 431 by the aid of 'correct copies' from Constantinople. Streeter[4] maintains that the Greek MSS used in the revision were of the fam. Θ type.

The Text. Streeter thinks that provisionally the Armenian may be regarded as a supplementary witness for the fam. Θ text. C. S. C. Williams[5] points out that until a critical edition of the Armenian New Testament is available the amount of 'Caesarean' support given by the version is difficult to assess.

Important Features.

Mk. xvi. 9–20 is omitted by three of the earliest MSS, but is found in the Edschmiadzin MS (A.D. 989) with the note 'Of the presbyter Ariston'.

Lk. xxii. 43f is omitted by three early MSS, but is found in the earliest.

Jn. vii. 53–viii. 11 is omitted by the earliest MSS, but is found in the Edschmiadzin MS.

THE GEORGIAN VERSION (geo). This version was in use in the Iberian Church in the Caucasus. It is sometimes called the Iberian Version. It was based on the Armenian, but an

---

[1] Kenyon, *The Text of the Greek Bible*, 134.

[2] So J. A. Robinson, *Euthaliana*, Texts and Studies, iii, 3 (1895), 72–91.

[3] See the works cited by C. S. C. Williams, McNeile's *Introduction*, 412,

[4] Streeter, *Op. cit.*, 104f.   [5] *Op. cit.*, 412.

early form of the Armenian influenced by the fam. Θ text.
R. P. Blake has produced the Georgian text of Mark and
Matthew and later that of John.[1] In a lecture entitled
'Twenty-Five Years of Theological Study' delivered at the
University of Manchester in 1929 F. C. Burkitt spoke of
Blake's edition of the text of Mark as 'almost the equivalent
of a third MS of the Old Syriac'.[2]

Georgian MSS. The earliest and best is the Adysh (geo[1])
written in A.D. 897. Other MSS (geo[2] A, B) are the Opiza
MS (913) and the Tbet' MS (995).

The Text. There appears to be wide agreement that the
Georgian text of Mark is Caesarean. Of the arguments of
Kirsopp Lake, Blake, and S. New[3] B. M. Metzger[4] writes,
'The authors correct, strengthen, and develop Streeter's
work on the Caesarean text, and (with the help of the
Armenian, Georgian, and Palestinian Syriac) reconstruct the
Caesarean text of Mark, chapters 1, 6, and 11.' It is of
interest to note that Mk. xvi. 9–20 is omitted by the earliest
Georgian MSS (the Adysh and Opiza MSS), but is found in
the Tbet' MS. It is added as a kind of Appendix to the
Four Gospels after John.

The Date. The date of the version is not certain but may
be as early as the fifth century.

THE ETHIOPIC VERSION (aeth). Christianity became the
national religion of Abyssinia about the end of the fifth
century. A translation would manifestly soon be needed
and the date of the version is probably the fifth or sixth
century. The existing MSS are very late, the oldest being
of the thirteenth century. They are not therefore of much
value for textual purposes.

[1] *Patrologia Orientalis*, xx, 3 (1929) 435–574, xxiv, 1 (1933) 1–168,
xxvi, 4 (1950).   [2] *Bulletin of John Rylands Library*, xiv, 1, 47.
    [3] 'The Caesarean Text of the Gospel of Mark,' *HTR*, 21 (1928),
207–404.
    [4] *Studies and Documents*, xvi (*Annotated Bibliography of the Textual
Criticism of the New Testament*), 93.

D

The Text. The text is said to be based on Greek MSS with traces of an earlier version dependent on the Old Syriac.

THE GOTHIC VERSION (goth). This version was made for the Goths of the Danubian provinces by Bishop Ulfilas (Wulfila, 'Little Wolf') who died *c.* A.D. 380. It contains parts of the Gospels and the Pauline Epistles (but not Heb.). The text is of the α type with β and δ readings. The best MS is Codex Argenteus at Upsala (fifth or sixth century). It is a handsome MS written in silver on purple vellum.

THE ARABIC VERSIONS (arab). These raise many questions. The MSS are late but plentiful and the text is mixed (Greek, Syriac, and Coptic in origin). They are useless for critical purposes.

VII

PATRISTIC AND OTHER EARLY QUOTATIONS

THE value of these quotations[1] is that they serve to indicate the kind of text used by the writer in question. They also help us to *localize* and *date* readings and types of text in the MSS and Versions. For example, 'Jesus Barabbas' which as we have seen is read by Θ fam. 1 sy[s] [pal] arm, is attested also by Origen who died in A.D. 253. The reading therefore was current in the first half of the third century, and perhaps earlier, at Caesarea, Alexandria, and Antioch. At the same time, however, Patristic quotations need to be used with care.

Principles affecting the Use of Early Quotations. First, the true text of the writer has to be ascertained. Like the New Testament MSS the writings of the Fathers were subject to scribal corruption. Moreover, the text of a quotation was not infrequently assimilated to that of later MSS (e.g. the Vulgate). In judging between two alternative readings the principle to be adopted is that the one which *diverges* from the later ecclesiastical text (the TR) is more likely to be original. But there is absolute certainty only when the context of the quotation is decisive.

Secondly, the question has always to be considered whether the writer is quoting from a MS or from memory. Manifestly, the evidence is at its best if we can be reasonably sure that a

---

[1] The Fathers have usually been read either in the Benedictine editions or in Migne's *Patrologia*. These are based on few and late MSS. Critical texts are now provided in the *Corpus of Latin Ecclesiastical Writers* (The Imperial Academy of Vienna) and the *Corpus of Greek Ecclesiastical Writers* (The Academy of Berlin).

MS is being used. This is more probable in the case of longer quotations. Shorter quotations were often made from memory, and memory sometimes plays strange tricks. An example given by Dr. Salmon is often quoted[1] from more modern times. Jeremy Taylor uses Jn. iii. 3, 'Except a man be born again, he cannot see the kingdom of God,' nine times, but only twice alike and never correctly.

Thirdly, the presence of *conflate* readings is to be noted, that is, readings which combine two or more variants in order to obtain a smooth and well-rounded text.

It will be seen that the use of Patristic quotations is subject to severe limitations. Nevertheless, for the reasons given this kind of evidence is of great value and importance both in itself and for its bearing upon the history of the New Testament text.

Quotations from the Sub-Apostolic Age. Until about A.D. 150 the quotations are of little value for textual purposes. They can be studied in the Epistle of Barnabas, the Didache, I Clement, the Epistles of Ignatius and Polycarp, the *Shepherd* of Hermas, and the homily known as 2 Clement.[2] From A.D. 150–75 evidence of value is forthcoming, but it is scanty and fragmentary. It is found in quotations assigned by Church Fathers to Marcion, in the writings of Justin Martyr, and in the *Diatessaron* of Tatian. The text is mainly of the δ type. After this period the evidence is full and explicit and is representative of various parts of the Church.

Quotations from the End of the Second Century Onwards. Only the most important of the Fathers and other writers can be mentioned here and the character of the text used by them.

1. ALEXANDRIA

Clement of Alexandria (d. 212 or 220) was Head of the Catechetical School from about 190 to 203. He was the

---

[1] See Kenyon, *Handbook*, 207.
[2] See *The New Testament in the Apostolic Fathers* (1905) by a Committee of the Oxford Society of Historical Theology.

author of important works including the *Stromateis* (Patches) in eight books. His quotations are of the δ type akin to the text of the Old Latin and the Old Syriac.

Origen (d. 253) has been described as 'the first textual critic of the New Testament'.[1] Born about 185 he succeeded Clement in 203, but after 231 lived at Caesarea. Origen compiled the Hexapla, which contained six forms of the Old Testament text, wrote many New Testament commentaries, compared MSS, and discussed variant readings. His quotations represent a mixed kind of text mainly of the β type but sometimes of the δ type. Streeter maintains that a change in the character of his text is visible after his departure from Alexandria to Caesarea and thus he becomes an authority for the text of fam. Θ.

2. ROME AND GAUL. See the references made above to Justin Martyr, Marcion, and Tatian, all of whom spent a considerable period in Rome and whose quotations are of the δ type.

Irenaeus (d. about 202). Irenaeus was born in Asia Minor where he saw and heard Polycarp. Later he went to Rome and then to Lyons where he became Bishop until his death. His principal work is *The Refutation and Subversion of Falsely-named Gnosis* described by Jerome as *Adversus omnes haereses* which he wrote about 185. His quotations are of the δ type represented by Codex Bezae.

Hippolytus (d. 236). Hippolytus lived in or near Rome and in Sardinia. He wrote many works including the *Philosophumena* or *Refutation of all the Heresies* and the *Defence of the Gospel and Apocalypse of John*. His quotations are of the δ type.

3. AFRICA (Carthage)
Tertullian (d. about 220). Tertullian was a presbyter of Carthage at one time resident in Rome. He became a

---

[1] Kenyon, *Handbook*, 214.

Montanist in 203. His quotations are sometimes from a Latin MS and sometimes from a Greek MS and are mainly of the δ type resembling Codex Veronensis[1] (b) and Codex Bezae (D). Kenyon[2] says his evidence must be used with caution.

Cyprian (martyred in 258). Cyprian was Bishop of Carthage from 248 to 258. His quotations are of the δ type. Apparently he used a MS practically identical with Codex Bobiensis (k).

Augustine (d. 430). Augustine was Bishop of Hippo in Numidia 395–430. In his earlier writings his text represents the Old Latin, but after 400 he used the Vulgate for longer quotations.

4. SYRIA (Antioch)

Aphraates was Bishop in a monastery near Nineveh about 340. He wrote homilies in Syriac. His Gospel quotations appear to be taken from the *Diatessaron*.

Ephraem (d. 373) was a later contemporary of Aphraates. F. C. Burkitt[3] has shown that in his New Testament quotations he used the *Diatessaron* and not the Peshitta.

5. CAESAREA.

As already indicated Streeter has argued that the fam. Θ text is represented in the later writings of Origen.

Origen (d. 253) appears to have used this text after his removal to Caesarea in 231.

Eusebius (d. *c.* 340) was Bishop of Caesarea for twenty-seven years and wrote many works and commentaries. Since Streeter wrote his *Four Gospels*[4] (1924) Kirsopp Lake[5] has shown that in Mark Eusebius also used the fam. Θ text.

---

[1] Cf. W. Sanday, *The Gospels of the Second Century*, 342.
[2] *Handbook*, 216.   [3] *Evangelion da-Mepharreshe*, ii, 112ff.
[4] Fourth Impression (1926), 91.
[5] 'The Caesarean Text of the Gospel of Mark', *HTR*, 21 (1928), 207–404, K. Lake, R. P. Blake, and S. New.

6. BYZANTIUM. The text current in Byzantium in the fourth century is represented by the quotations of Chrysostom.

Chrysostom (d. 407), born at Antioch (*c.* 347), lived there till 398 when he became Patriarch. His quotations in his voluminous commentaries show the α text firmly established. They reveal signs of the δ text, but none of the β text. The same type of text was used by the later Greek Fathers, including Theodoret (d. 458) and John of Damascus (d. 750), and on throughout the Middle Ages. This text, the Textus Receptus, appears in the first printed editions of the Greek Testament and it is followed in the Authorized Version.

It will be seen that the evidence supplied by the quotations of the Fathers and other early writers is of the greatest importance. It clearly shows (1) that the δ text was almost universal in its range in the second and third centuries, (2) that the β text and the later Caesarean texts emerged in the third century and may even have existed at an earlier date, and (3) that the α text was current from the beginning of the fourth century, remaining supreme in ecclesiastical use until comparatively modern times. These facts constitute one of the key arguments in the textual theory of Westcott and Hort.

VIII

PRINTED EDITIONS OF THE
GREEK NEW TESTAMENT

THE first printed edition of the Greek New Testament was completed by Cardinal Ximenes in 1514 in the Complutensian Polyglot. It was not published until 1522 and in the meanwhile Erasmus, the Reformer, commissioned by the printer Froben of Basle, rapidly prepared an edition and published it in 1516. In this task he used the few MSS to hand in Basle, the good minuscule MS 1 and the MS 2 which is a late copy of the Byzantine text. The MS used for the Apocalypse lacked the last six verses and these he retranslated from the Latin. In his third edition of 1522 he introduced the passage about the Three Heavenly Witnesses (I Jn. v. 7f, AV) from the late MS 61. This passage he had omitted in the first edition because it was not present in the MSS then at his disposal.

From 1546 onwards the successive editions of Robert Stephanus appeared, largely based on the Greek text of Erasmus. A revision of this text by the Reformer Beza was printed in the handsome Elzevir editions from 1624 onwards. It is this Stephanus-Elzevir text which is known as the *Textus Receptus*, or the Received Text, from the famous phrase in the second edition of 1633, *Textum ergo habes nunc ab omnibus receptum*, now often indicated in textual notes by the symbol ς. This text is embodied in the Authorized Version and remained in general use until the Westcott and Hort edition of 1881.

Meantime valuable textual work was done by a series of British scholars in the seventeenth and eighteenth centuries including B. Walton, J. Fell, J. Mill, R. Bentley, E. Wells, who collated MSS and discussed readings. Later similar work was done by a number of German scholars, including J. J. Wetstein, J. A. Bengel, J. S. Semler, J. J. Griesbach, and in the nineteenth century by C. Lachmann, C. Tischendorf, and others.

Fell printed the Elzevir edition and supplied with it an *apparatus criticus*. Mill did the same with the text of Stephanus and discussed critical principles. Bentley put forward proposals for an edition which were not fulfilled but left valuable textual materials bequeathed to Trinity College, Cambridge. His former asistant, J. J. Wetstein, was the first to introduce the system of manuscript notation which with subsequent modifications is still in use. Bengel, who produced an edition in 1734, laid a foundation for further advance by dividing the textual witnesses into two families, the Asiatic containing the mass of later MSS and the African in which he placed A and a few other MSS and versions. Semler distinguished three classes, the Alexandrian, the Oriental, and the Occidental, and this scheme was extended by his pupil, Griesbach, who classified the MSS belonging to the three families: the Alexandrian (represented by C L 1 13 33 69 bo sy[h] arm aeth Clem. Or. and Eus.), the Western (D the O. Lat. some min. and Fathers), and the Constantinopolitan (A and most later Greek MSS). The significance of the classification is seen when it is remembered that at the time B was little known and א was not yet discovered.[1] 'It will be seen,' writes Kenyon, 'how nearly Griesbach's theory anticipated that which holds the field among New Testament students to-day.'[2]

A new period begins with C. Lachmann who published the first of his two editions in 1831 basing it upon the most ancient authorities to the exclusion of the mass of later MSS. C. Tischendorf also rendered invaluable service, not only in

[1] Cf. Kenyon, *The Text of the Greek Bible*, 161.
[2] *Handbook*, 240.

the discovery and editing of Codex Sinaiticus, but in transcribing and collating many MSS, and, above all, in publish-
ing the eighth edition of his Greek Testament with its
remarkably full *apparatus criticus* (1869–72). Two English
scholars must also be mentioned among the predecessors of
Westcott and Hort, S. P. Tregelles and F. H. A. Scrivener.
Tregelles began in 1838 to prepare an edition based on the
most important ancient MSS. He also collated all the most
important MSS in Europe. His edition appeared in parts
during the years 1857 to 1872. Although Scrivener did not
produce an edition, he collated MSS and published the text
of Stephanus with readings from Lachmann, Tischendorf,
and Tregelles. He also wrote his *Plain Introduction to the
Criticism of the New Testament* (1861, 4th ed. 1894) which
long remained a standard work.

It will be seen that Westcott and Hort stand in a noble
succession of scholars from whom they learned much and to
whom they paid generous tribute. In particular, they
declared that they venerated the name of Griesbach above
that of every other textual critic of the New Testament.[1]
In their opinion he and his predecessors failed to apprehend
in its true magnitude the part played by mixture in the
history of the text during the fourth and following centuries,
and they too readily identified Alexandrian readings with
those preserved wholly or chiefly at Alexandria. They also
thought that Griesbach gave a dangerously disproportionate
weight to internal evidence and especially to transcriptional
probability, but they recognized that these limitations of
view were the natural result of the slenderness of the available materials.[2] Of Tischendorf and Tregelles they wrote,
'Their indefatigable labours in the discovery and exposition
of fresh evidence, aided by similar research on the part of
others, provide all who come after them with invaluable
resources not available half a century ago.'[3]

[1] *The New Testament in the Original Greek*, ii, 185.
[2] *Ibid.*   [3] *Op. cit.*, 13f.

Westcott and Hort's edition of the Greek text appeared in 1881. The Prolegomena was written by Hort, but it embodied the joint conclusions of the two scholars. The Introduction, with an Appendix containing Notes on Select Readings and Notes on Orthography, appeared in the following year. It is introduced by the words, 'This edition is an attempt to present exactly the original words of the New Testament, so far as they can now be determined from surviving documents.'[1] Its influence has been immense and far-reaching, and it still needs to be read by the advanced student. Although subsequent discoveries have led to modifications in their theory, the Introduction remains the standard work on textual criticism since much for which they contended has stood the test of time.

Other editions of the Greek Testament published since that of Westcott and Hort may with advantage be mentioned at this point. One of these is A. Souter's *Novum Testamentum Graece*[2] published at Oxford in 1910 which is supplied with a select *apparatus* containing the more important variants of the principal MSS, versions, and Fathers. The Greek text represents that found in English in the Revised Version of 1881. Another is the edition prepared by the late Eberhard Nestle for the *Würtembergische Bibelanstalt* in 1898 and now reissued by his son, Dr. Erwin Nestle, and Dr. Kurt Aland in its twenty-fifth edition (1956). The text is based on the the texts of Tischendorf, Westcott and Hort, and B. Weiss, and where these differ, the text of the two who agree is followed in the main. The *apparatus* includes readings from Westcott and Hort and H. von Soden, together with readings

---

[1] *Op. cit.*, I.

[2] Mention also must be made of the colossal task undertaken by S. C. E. Legg in his *Nouum Testamentum Graece secundum Textum Westcotto-Hortianum* of which the sections on Mark (1935) and Matthew (1940) have already appeared, a task which after discussions and criticisms is still in progress. See E. C. Colwell, *Classical Philology*, 33 (1938), 112–15, G. D. Kilpatrick, *JTS*, xliii, 30–4, T. W. Manson, *JTS*, xliii, 83–92.

from the newly discovered MSS, W, Θ, and the Papyri. Yet another is that of H. J. Vogels (1920, 2nd ed. 1922) in which the text frequently agrees with that of von Soden in spite of the editor's independent views. Finally, mention must be made of the British and Foreign Bible Society's text founded on that of Nestle. To mark its 150th Anniversary the Society issued a second edition in 1958 prepared by Professor G. D. Kilpatrick of Queen's College, Oxford, after some years of collaboration with Dr. Erwin Nestle. A useful Introduction is supplied and a simplified but up-to-date *apparatus* of very great value to students of the text.

A summary such as the above is apt to read like a catalogue, but if we read it with imagination, we cannot fail to be impressed by the sustained progress which has been made throughout the last three centuries in the Universities and parsonages of Europe. In all the literature of the world no book has received a tithe of the devoted study and research bestowed upon the New Testament. And research still continues as new MSS come to hand and as the relationships of the MSS and versions are repeatedly examined.

IX

THE TEXTUAL THEORY OF
WESTCOTT AND HORT

THE textual theory of Westcott and Hort must now be considered because of its importance in itself and because of its fundamental bearing upon any further advance which may be made in textual criticism in the future. There are many excellent summaries of their theory, notably that of A. H. M'Neile in his *Introduction to the New Testament* (1927, 2nd ed. revised by C. S. C. Williams, 1953), but it is studied best in their own words in the second volume of their great work, *The New Testament in the Original Greek* (1882).

Westcott and Hort's argument is progressive. They begin by considering the critic's procedure when confronted by different readings in the MSS. *Intrinsic Probability* is the judgement formed from the decision which of two readings makes the best sense. Naturally the trained reader has an advantage over the untrained, but even so, competent observers will differ in their decisions since the original writers are not always grammatical, clear, or consistent. *Transcriptional Probability* therefore must also be considered, that is, the consideration about what the copyist is likely to have written, having regard to the known types of corruption in the copying of MSS. This test again is subject to uncertainty, but the two processes are undoubtedly of value when the nature of the documents in which various readings are found is determined. Westcott and Hort lay down the principle that 'knowledge of documents should precede final judgement upon readings'.[1] The next step is to consider the

_____
[1] *Op. cit.*, 31.

documents in their historical relationships. 'All trustworthy restoration of corrupted texts', they observe, 'is founded on the study of their history.'[1] Manuscripts must be grouped and considered from the standpoint of their *genealogy*. If, let us say, of ten MSS nine agree against one, but the nine have a common original, it is simply a question of one reading against another. In tracing the genealogy of MSS complications occasioned by the mixture of texts have to be borne in mind. The clearest evidence of this is afforded by 'conflate' readings, that is, combinations of readings into a composite whole by mere addition or fusion. Of this possibility, which is closely connected with their textual theory, Westcott and Hort say, 'Where we find a variation with three variants, two of them simple alternatives to each other, and the third a combination of the other two, there is usually a strong presumption that the third is the latest and due to mixture, not the third the earliest and the other two due to independent impulses of simplification.'[2] We thus learn to set a special value on those documents which rarely or never support conflate readings, as witnesses to texts antecedent to mixture. The application of the genealogical method helps us to set aside readings that cannot be right and enables us to estimate the Internal Evidence of Groups of MSS.

Principles adopted by Westcott and Hort. These may be summarized as follows: (1) Of individual readings the most probable is that which best explains the origin of its rivals; (2) The knowledge of documents must precede a final judgement upon divergent readings; (3) Authorities must be grouped in families of MSS descended from a common ancestor; (4) The character of the groups must be estimated.

The Principal Texts according to Westcott and Hort

These have already been mentioned in the chapter on Notation and Types of Text, but the distribution must be repeated because this is a vital element in their textual theory. Westcott and Hort distinguish: (1) the great mass

---

[1] *Op. cit.*, 40.   [2] *Op. cit.*, 49.

of later MSS and cursives, together with syᵖ and the later Fathers, which in their view attest the *Syrian* or Antiochian text of the late third and fourth centuries (the α type); (2) A smaller group, including ℵ B 33 bo, etc., representing the *Neutral* text (β); (3) a type, not found in any one MS, but reflected in readings in ℵ C L 33 bo, which they name the *Alexandrian text* (γ); (4) a group, represented by D 28 565 the Old Latin the Old Syriac and sa containing the *Western* text (δ).

The History of the Text in Westcott and Hort's View

Before describing Westcott and Hort's arguments it will be of advantage to summarize their account of the history of the text.

1. In their opinion corruption began early, especially in the Gospels. This corruption consisted of expansions, omissions, and assimilations of one passage to another. Hence there arose a type of text which departed widely from the original tradition. They think that this text took root in the Syriac Church and was carried westwards, and accordingly they call it the 'Western' Text. In their view a reading wholly or mainly Western is to be regarded with the utmost suspicion. The exception is the Western omissions mainly in Lk. xxii and xxiv. Since the prevailing tendency of this text is to make additions, its omissions preserve the original text.

2. Meantime, they submit, another kind of modification, mainly in matters of grammar and syntax, was taking place at Alexandria. This text they call the Alexandrian text.

3. Later, in the third and fourth centuries, when the divergencies in the manuscripts became more marked, an authoritative revision, they infer, was undertaken. Its aims were (1) to combine different readings, and (2) to produce an easy and flowing text. This revision, they suggest, was produced at or near Antioch, possibly by Lucian of Antioch in two stages, in A.D. 300 or thereabouts and A.D. 350. This

text they call the Syrian Text. It rapidly gained popularity, since it was smooth, full, and readable, and it is the text of the overwhelming majority of later uncials, minuscules, and versions.

4. The best text, in their opinion, is the 'Neutral Text' attested by ℵ and B. This combination is very strong, and, they believe, the common ancestor of these manuscripts cannot be far removed from the autographs. No reading of B, they insist, apart from obvious slips, can safely be passed over, and in most cases its testimony is decisive. With a few exceptions, which they mention, Westcott and Hort say, 'It is our belief (1) that the readings of ℵ B should be accepted as the true readings until strong internal evidence is found to the contrary, and (2) that no readings of ℵ B can safely be rejected absolutely, though it is sometimes right to place them only on an alternative footing, especially where they receive no support from Versions or Fathers.'[1]

The Basis of Westcott and Hort's Theory

Westcott and Hort base their estimate of the Syrian text as later than the Western, Neutral, and Alexandrian texts on three main arguments: (1) the analysis of conflate readings, (2) the Ante-Nicene Patristic evidence, and (3) the Internal Evidence of Syrian readings.[2] Of these the first two are the most important.

(1) The Analysis of Conflate Readings

Eight conflate readings are examined which point to the later origin of the Syrian text: Mk. vi. 33, viii. 26, ix. 38, ix. 49, Lk. ix. 10, xi. 54, xii. 18, xxiv. 53. The conflate reading, they argue, appears in the α text which simply combines the β and δ readings. Two of these are here presented in a simplified form for purposes of illustration. All of them should be read in the much fuller form in which Westcott and Hort present them.

Mk. ix. 49. The three readings with the authorities which attest them are as follows:

---
[1] *Op. cit.*, 225.   [2] *Op. cit.*, 93–115.

1. πᾶς γὰρ πυρὶ ἁλισθήσεται is read by ℵ B L W fam. 1
565 700 *et al* sy⁸ sa bo geo arm and is represented in the RV
and RSV.

2. πᾶσα γὰρ θυσία ἁλὶ ἁλισθήσεται: D a b c d ff *et al.*

3. πᾶς γὰρ πυρὶ ἁλισθήσεται καὶ πᾶσα θυσία ἁλὶ ἁλισθήσεται:
A C Θ *al pler* fam. 13 28 892 1071 *al pler* f q r vg syᵖ ʰ aeth.
cf. AV. Of these three readings it will be seen that the
first is the β text, the second the δ text, and that the third,
the α text, combines both.

Lk. xxiv. 53

1. εὐλογοῦντες τὸν θεόν: ℵ B C L bo (RV, RSV).

2. αἰνοῦντες τὸν θεόν: D a b vg Aug.

3. αἰνοῦντες καὶ εὐλογοῦντες τὸν θεόν: A and the mass of
MSS syᵖ (AV).

Again it is clear that the α reading is a conflation of the
others.

Commenting on the eight examples examined, Westcott
and Hort justly observe that a comparison of them confirms
the conclusion that the longer readings are conflations of
two earlier readings.[1] On the other hand no such readings
are found in the α text. 'To the best of our belief,' they say,
'the relations . . . are never inverted.'[2] This argument is
very cogent indeed.

(2) *Ante-Nicene Patristic evidence*

Westcott and Hort's second argument is that no reading
strictly belonging to the α family is found in any Father
before Chrysostom whereas the β, γ, and δ types are attested
in Fathers of an earlier date. The β and γ types appear in
Clement of Alexandria, Origen, and Eusebius, although at
times the δ type is found in these Fathers. Among those who
use the δ text are Justin Martyr, Tatian, Irenaeus, Tertullian,
Hippolytus, and Cyprian. Before the middle of the third
century, at the very earliest, we have no signs of distinctively Syrian readings. 'This is a fact of great significance,
ascertained as it is exclusively by external evidence, and

[1] *Op. cit.,* 104f.   [2] *Op. cit.,* 106.

E

therefore supplying an absolutely independent verification
and extension of the result already obtained by comparison
of the internal character of readings as classified by conflation.'[1]

(3) *Internal Evidence of Syrian readings*

Westcott and Hort claim that when distinctively Syrian
readings are minutely compared with the rival variants,
their claim to be regarded as original readings is found
gradually to diminish, and at last to disappear.[2] From this
it follows that they may be set aside as corruptions of the
apostolic text.[3] Since it is based on internal evidence this
judgement is subjective, but when considered along with the
other two arguments it is weighty.

The Value of Westcott and Hort's Theory

Westcott and Hort's arguments as set out above have
compelling force, and in its main submissions their theory
is generally accepted. It was vigorously opposed, but unsuc-
cessfully, by Dean J. B. Burgon and Prebendary E. Miller[4].
Westcott and Hort's view of the α text is sound, but the
name 'Syrian' or 'Antiochian' is not the best. Their high
opinion of the β text is justified, but not to the neglect of
other texts which sometimes deserve preference. The β
text is not an immediate descendant of the original text,
but a careful revision undertaken at Alexandria about the
beginning of the third century. 'Neutral' is too optimistic
a name for this text, and since the γ text is generally regarded
as an editorial revision of the β type, Streeter's suggestion
that we should use the name 'Alexandrian' instead of
'Neutral' is a distinct improvement. Further discoveries
show how excellent this text is, even if it does not warrant
the exclusive priority Westcott and Hort assigned to it. In
recording a list of twenty-eight papyrus fragments made

[1] *Op. cit.*, 115.   [2] *Op. cit.*, 116.
[3] *Op. cit.*, 117.
[4] *The Traditional Text of the Holy Gospels vindicated and established*
(1896), *The Causes of the Corruption of the Traditional Text of the
Holy Gospels* (1896).

available during the decade 1941–51 B. M. Metzger[1] observed that the overwhelming majority of them belong to the β type of text, so that to the handful of MSS of the fourth to the eighth century 'there must now be added about a score of other witnesses'. It is now seen, he says, that the Alexandrian family was not a narrow and slender rivulet, but was widely prevalent in Egypt and extended also to southern Palestine.[2]

It is as regards the δ text that the greatest progress has been made. This text is much more valuable than Westcott and Hort supposed. As we shall see in studying Streeter's textual views, it is no longer regarded as a single family, but as a widely extended group with the result that the distribution of our textual witnesses is considerably extended. These developments are due mainly to further detailed study of the 'Western' text and to the discovery of MSS and versions which were not known to Westcott and Hort. They are occasioned also by the further investigation of the versions, the Old Syriac by F. C. Burkitt, the Sahidic by G. Horner, the Armenian and the Georgian by R. P. Blake, the researches in the minuscule MSS by K. Lake, S. New, and others, and the study of the wide influence of the Old Syriac on the early versions by A. Vööbus.[3]

Among the manuscripts and versions discovered since Westcott and Hort's edition of 1881 are the Sinaitic Syriac MS, the Koridethi MS, the Freer MS, the Chester Beatty Papyri, P[52], Papyrus Bodmer II, and the twenty-eight fragments mentioned above in the article of B. M. Metzger. It is remarkable that, in spite of these additions to our knowledge, so much of Westcott and Hort's theory still stands as a contribution of permanent value to textual criticism.

[1] See *ET*, lxiii, 309–11, 'Recently Published Fragments of the Greek New Testament.'
[2] *Op. cit.*, 311.
[3] *Early Versions of the New Testament* (1955).

No one has done more to bring out the significance of the discovery of W, Θ, sy[s], fam. 1 and fam. 13 in their bearing upon Westcott and Hort's theory than B. H. Streeter, and to his textual views we now turn.

X

THE CONTRIBUTION OF
B. H. STREETER

PART I of Streeter's book *The Four Gospels*[1] discusses 'The Manuscript Tradition'. The discussion is one of entrancing interest and, after making himself familiar with the Westcott and Hort theory, the student ought to make it the subject of diligent study. The distinctive themes are Streeter's views regarding Local Texts, the Caesarean Text, and suggestions concerning the method of citing textual authorities, omissions, and assimilations.

Relation to the Westcott and Hort Theory. Streeter accepts Westcott and Hort's estimate of the α text, but gives it the name the Byzantine text because it was the standard text of the Byzantine Empire from the fourth century and throughout the Middle Ages. To the β text he assigns the name the Alexandrian text and rejects the γ text as representing a separate family. He breaks up the δ text into four families, the Western text proper consisting of the text of Italy and Gaul and that of Carthage, and the Eastern including the texts of Antioch and Caesarea. With their principal representatives these texts are as follows:

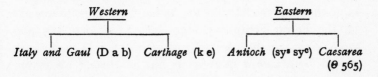

Western		*Eastern*	
Italy and Gaul (D a b)	*Carthage* (k e)	*Antioch* (sy^s sy^c)	*Caesarea* (θ 565)

[1] Of this work F. C. Burkitt wrote, 'I venture to think "The Four Gospels" the most important book that has been written upon its august subject for half a generation,' *JTS*, xxvi (1924–5), 278–94.

Local Texts. Streeter emphasized the immense importance
of the early local texts current at the great centres of
Christianity. He argued that in a given area copies would
be corrected by one another, and especially by those in use
at the principal Churches, Byzantium, Antioch, Caesarea,
Alexandria, Carthage, and Rome. The growing veneration
for the text as inspired would result in the tendency to
lay more and more stress on the importance of an accurate
text. 'This would naturally result in the smaller churches
obtaining new copies from the greater metropolitan sees,
since these would be thought likely to possess a pure text. . . .
Thus the local texts of smaller churches would tend to become assimilated to those of the greater centres in their
immediate neighbourhood.'[1]   Streeter claims that the
high road of textual criticism is (1) to recover the local texts
of the great churches, and (2) to work back to a common
original that will explain them all.[2] He holds that the work
is greatly simplified by the fact that readings later than the
fifth century can be ignored, except when they differ from
the prevailing Byzantine text. He formulates a canon of
first importance in the words, *'Of MSS., whether Greek or
Latin, later than the fifth century, only those readings need be
noted which differ from the standard text.'*[3]

Among other principles Streeter says, *'The precedence of
MSS depends, not on their age, but on their pedigree.'*[4] He
warns us against the illusion that the testimony of uncials is
necessarily greater than that of minuscules. The leading
MSS are B, ℵ, D, L, and Θ, but there are several cursives
quite as important as A, C, and W, and of decidedly greater
value than any uncial after the first eight. Among these are
33, the Ferrar group (13, etc.), fam. 1, 28, 700, 565, and
579. *'Research into the pedigree of a MS.'*, he maintains,
'should begin with a study of its text of Mark,'[5] his reason

---

[1] *Op. cit.*, 38.   [2] *Op. cit.*, 39.
[3] *Op. cit.*, 44. The italics as in all these quotations are Streeter's.
[4] *Op. cit.*, 50.   [5] *Op. cit.*, 64.

being that Mark has escaped Byzantine revision in more copies and to a greater extent than the other Gospels.

The Texts of the Great Sees. Rome, Alexandria, and Antioch were 'the frontier stations of Greek-speaking Christianity'. There is therefore a presumption that the Latin, Egyptian, and Syriac versions were derived from Greek texts current in these centres.

The Text of Alexandria

By this text Streeter understands Westcott and Hort's β text. He is inclined to believe that it is the result of a revision undertaken by Hesychius, an Egyptian bishop who was martyred in A.D. 307.[1] As we have seen, he explains the γ text as a degenerate form of this text caused by the accidents of copying and additions from older texts.

The chief authorities for the text of Alexandria are B, ℵ, L, 33, bo, sa (in the main), Origen (before A.D. 231), and Cyril of Alexandria (d. A.D. 444). Any reading of B supported by ℵ, L, etc., he claims, 'almost certainly belongs to the Alexandrian text in its earliest form.'[2]

The Text of Antioch

Streeter accepts the view of F. C. Burkitt that the Greek text underlying the Old Syriac version was derived from the older text of Antioch. Hence he takes, as representing the second century text of Antioch, sy[s], sy[c], and sy[p] when it differs from the Byzantine text.

The Text of Caesarea

The advocacy of this local text is the distinctive contribution of Streeter to textual criticism. In forming his views he was strongly influenced by the joint article of R. P. Blake and Kirsopp Lake in the *Harvard Theological Review* for July 1923,[3] 'The Text of the Gospels and the Koridethi Codex'. Streeter describes the discovery of this codex as 'comparable in importance to that of ℵ or the Sinaitic Syriac' because it enables us to see the real connexion between fam. 1, fam. 13, 28, 565, and 700, which, as Lake

---

[1] *Op. cit.*, 121–7.   [2] *Op. cit.*, 127.   [3] 16 (1923), 267–86.

argued, form in reality a single family,[1] fam. Θ. This family is almost equidistant from both the Alexandrian and Western texts. Streeter presents detailed evidence for this conclusion, maintaining in particular that the text of fam. Θ is that of Origen and Eusebius.

The argument that Origen is an authority for the fam. Θ text is so interesting and important that it must be described more fully.[2] It is based upon the text of Mark used in Origen's *Commentary on John*, his *Commentary on Matthew*, and his *Exhortation to Martyrdom*.

In books i–x of the *Commentary on John*, Streeter argues, Origen quotes the greater part of Mk. i. 1–27 and the whole of Mk. xi. 1–12, using in the main the Alexandrian text, but in the later books his text agrees with that of fam. Θ.[3] The Θ text is also used in the two later works mentioned above, the *Commentary on Matthew* and the *Exhortation to Martyrdom*, both of which belong entirely to the period when Origen lived in Caesarea. Streeter thinks that fam. Θ represents a text already in existence when he moved to Caesarea, and not a recension made subsequently by himself. 'We conclude,' he writes, 'that fam. Θ represents the text which Origen found already established in the Church of Caesarea in 231.'[4] 'This,' he adds, 'affords another fixed point for the history of the text of the New Testament.'[5]

Streeter's conclusions were subsequently strengthened by the further study of W (the Freer MS), which has been shown to have a Western text in Mk. i–v. 30, but in Mk. v. 31–xvi. 8 an increase of the number of agreements with fam. 1, fam. 13, 565 and 28, i.e. a Caesarean text.[6] Still further support was afforded when the Chester Beatty MS P[45] was discovered and examined. 'In Mark,' writes Kenyon, 'the important fact emerges that the papyrus ranges itself with

[1] *Op. cit.*, 79f.
[2] Cf. Streeter, *op. cit.*, 79–107, 572–89, 598–600.
[3] *Op. cit.*, 93–102.   [4] *Op. cit.*, 101.
[5] *Op. cit.*, 102.
[6] Cf. Streeter, in Appendix V added in the 1926 reprint, 598–600.

the Caesarean group.' The manuscript with which it shows the closest affinity is the Freer MS at Washington (W). Next to this comes Fam. 13, then Cod. 565, Fam. 1, and Θ, and then Cod. 700.[1]

The case for the existence of this text is manifestly very strong. Kenyon says, 'Henceforward the Caesarean text has an assured place in textual criticism.'[2] In recent studies modifications and corrections have been suggested of which some account will be given in the following chapter.

The Text of Italy and Gaul

Streeter describes this text as 'a type of text at the furthest remove from that of B'.[3] Its principal representatives are D (Codex Bezae), the European Latin MSS a (Vercellensis), b (Veronensis), and the quotations of Tatian (c. 170) and Irenaeus (c. 185).

The Text of Carthage

This text is held by Streeter to be derived from an early form of Roman text.[4] It is represented by the African Latin MSS k (Bobiensis) and e (Palatinus) and the quotations of Cyprian (c. 250). In many readings it agrees with the Alexandrian MSS B and ℵ against the European Latin.[5] The fact that the text of k is to all intents and purposes identical with that of Cyprian is claimed by Streeter as another fixed point towards the determination of early local texts.

The Text of Byzantium

This is Westcott and Hort's α text, the Textus Receptus. It is represented by A (Alexandrinus) in the Gospels, E (Basiliensis), S (Vaticanus 354), and the mass of later uncials and minuscules, by the Syriac Peshitta (syp), the Gothic Version, Chrysostom (d. 407), and the later Fathers. Like Westcott and Hort Streeter thinks that it is an ecclesiastical revision by Lucian of Antioch (d. 312)[6] and was revised again later. This view is a conjecture, but so far as it goes

---

[1] *Recent Developments*, 57. [2] *Op. cit.*, 47. [3] *Op. cit.*, 67.
[4] *Op. cit.*, 66. [5] *Ibid.* [6] *Op. cit.*, 112–21.

it is supported by the fact that Chrysostom spent the greater part of his life at Antioch, and by the statement of Jerome in his Preface to the Vulgate version of Chronicles, that the Churches of Antioch approve the manuscripts containing the text of Lucian the martyr, while Alexandria and Egypt extol the authority of Hesychius.[1] The Gothic version is the first to show a predominantly Byzantine text, and it is perhaps significant that Ulfilas was consecrated Bishop in A.D. 341 at Antioch. The later Byzantine text appears to be related to the revision of Lucian in much the same way as the later Vulgate is related to Jerome's revision[2] and as the Alexandrian text in C L Δ Ψ 33, 579 is related to that of B.[3]

The Relationships between the Local Texts

Streeter's theory of Local Texts at the Great Sees has much cogency provided we do not define the texts too rigidly or regard them as self-contained. And this Streeter does not do. He points out that the five Churches of Alexandria, Caesarea, Antioch, Italy and Gaul, and Carthage stand in a circle round the Eastern Mediterranean in a graded series, and that each member is related to its next-door neighbour far more closely than to remoter members of the series. He puts his point as follows:

'Thus B (Alexandria) has much in common with *fam.* Θ (Caesarea); *fam.* Θ shares many striking readings with Syr. S (Antioch); Syr. S. in turn has contacts with D *b a* (Italy-Gaul); and, following round the circle to the point from which we started, *k* (Carthage) is in a sense a half-way house between D *b a* and B (Alexandria again).'[4]

He observes that antecedently we should rather expect the

---

[1] The passage runs: 'Alexandria et Aegyptus in Septuaginta suis Hesychium laudat auctorem, Constantinopolis usque Antiochiam Luciani Martyrii exemplaria probat, mediae inter has provinciae Palestinae codices legunt, quos ab Origene elaboratos Eusebius et Pamphilus vulgaverunt: totusque orbis hac inter se trifaria varietate compugnat.'

[2] *Op. cit.*, 113.   [3] *Op. cit.*, 125.   [4] *Op. cit.*, 106.

text of any particular locality to be, up to a point, inter-
mediate between the localities geographically contiguous
with it, but that 'the exactness of correspondence between
the geographical propinquity and the resemblance of text
exceeds anything we should have anticipated'.[1] This fact,
he claims, is of some weight in confirming the general thesis
propounded in these chapters.

The Right Method of Citing Textual Authorities

Following upon his views concerning local texts Streeter
maintains that the current practice of presenting evidence
by quoting (1) the uncials in alphabetical order and (2) the
cursives in arithmetical order, is fundamentally misleading.
It gives undue weight to the number of MSS which can be
cited, and supplies no clue to the relative importance of the
authorities which are cited. What we want to know is the
reading of (a) B ℵ and their allies, (b) of D and its allies,
(c) of the leading members of fam. Θ, (d) of the Old Syriac,
Armenian, and Old Georgian, and (e) of the T.R. It is
not necessary to cite further information, except where
the leading members of the groups disagree. This interesting
suggestion appears to over-simplify the scope of textual
procedure, and it has not been generally accepted except in
cases in which detailed evidence is not essential.

Omissions and Assimilation

Streeter draws attention to the submission of A. C. Clark[2]
that ancient scribes were most prone to accidental omission,
not interpolation. 'A text,' says Clark, 'is like a traveller
who loses a portion of his luggage every time he changes
trains.' The principle is sound, but qualifications are necessary in the case of Acts and the Gospels, because (1) B ℵ,
fam. Θ, sy[s], and k give good and ancient texts, and (2) oral
tradition supplied sayings which would be inserted in margins
and then in the text. An interesting suggestion is that

---

[1] *Ibid.*

[2] Cf. *The Descent of the Manuscripts* (1918), *The Primitive Text
of the Gospels and Acts* (1914), *JTS*, Jan. 1915, 226ff.

accidental omissions of an interesting kind would be most likely to be made good in the place where a Gospel was first produced. For example, since Luke and Acts were written in the west, B's omissions carry less weight than Western omissions. We shall be inclined to agree with Westcott and Hort in suspecting what they call 'Western non-inter-polations' in Luke because they are absent from the Roman text of Luke,[1] but hesitate to agree in rejecting passages for which the Western evidence is good, simply because they are absent from B. Similarly, if Matthew was written in Antioch, we shall look with special favour on any insertion attested by sy[s]. Streeter suggests that this principle works out well in practice in such cases as Mt. xxvii. 17,[2] 49, Lk. xxii. 43f, xxiii. 34. The two Lukan passages (The Agony and the prayer, 'Father forgive them. . . .') are omitted by Alexandrian and Eastern authorities (B W 579 sy[s], the latter also by Θ) and may have been omitted for doctrinal reasons.[3] The textual problems, however, are complicated, and the principle Streeter commends has to be considered in the light of the evidence as a whole.[4]

Assimilation of the texts of the Gospels to one another is, as Streeter observes,[5] the commonest of all forms of error, and perhaps the best known example is the expanded form of the Lord's Prayer in Lk. xi. 2–4. It is, however, one of the most difficult to check, since identical assimilations may have been made in different lines of transmission. There may be

[1] *Op. cit.*, 136. Streeter, however, accepts the genuineness of Lk. xxiv. 51, 'and he was taken up into heaven', which is one of Westcott and Hort's nine examples, on the ground that its omission in D and the Old Lat. may be an attempt to remove a contradiction between Luke and the Acts.

[2] Mt. xxvii. 17 is the passage in which 'Jesus Barabbas' is read in fam. Θ.

[3] Cf. Streeter, *op. cit.*, 137–9; C. S. C. Williams, *Alterations to the Text of the Synoptic Gospels and Acts*, 25–53.

[4] Although Lk. xxii. 43f is omitted by ℵ[a], it is read by ℵ* D, etc., and Lk. xxiii. 34 is read by ℵ* C L, etc. See the fuller discussion of these passages on p. 93f.   [5] *Op. cit.*, 139.

an avoidance of assimilation in Lk. iii. 22 where Streeter
accepts the Western reading, 'Thou art my Son, this day
have I begotten thee.'[1] All the local texts have suffered
from assimilation. Streeter contends that the tacit assump-
tion that B is practically immune from this type of corruption
has played havoc with the scientific study of the Synoptic
Problem.[2]

Conclusion

Streeter concludes that, although we may think that
Westcott and Hort relied too exclusively on the B text, and
that an 'eclectic' text based on the old local texts is a sounder
basis, the B ℵ text is the best of these and the one which,
in the main, a critical editor must follow. He summarizes
the local texts into:

An Egyptian, admirably preserved in ℵ B L;
an Italian and Gallic, represented with many corruptions,
    in D a b ff^2;
an African (perhaps = earlier Roman) found in k e (W^{mk});
an Antiochene, less adequately known to us through the
    Old Syriac;
a Caesarean, fairly well preserved in the non-Byzantine
    readings of fam. Θ (W^{mk}). (For W^{mk} see p. 17)

But the real need, he suggests, is for a thesaurus of various
readings bringing up to date Tischendorf's large edition of
1869. The text should be the Byzantine text, (1) since we
need to know the older texts which *differ* from this text, and
(2) because the apparatus itself would be enormously simplified. MSS, he thinks, should be cited in groups, Alexandrian,
Eastern, Western, and small print and small numbers and
letters above the line should be resolutely eschewed.

He observes that, though on minor points absolute
certainty may often be unobtainable, a text free from
serious modification or interpolation is guaranteed by the

[1] *Op. cit.*, 143, also C. S. C. Williams, *op. cit.*, 45–7.
[2] *Op. cit.*, 144.

concurrence of different lines of ancient and independent evidence. For the historian or general reader a text like that of Hort or Tischendorf, or that followed in the Revised Version, may be taken as reliable for ordinary purposes. 'But for fine points of scholarship, or when dealing with the Synoptic Problem, . . . it is vital to realise that in our search for the original reading we must, on occasion, go behind the printed texts.'[1]

In this chapter I have allowed Streeter to speak, as far as possible, for himself, and for the most part without comment, reserving criticisms and suggestions for the next chapter. Several points call for closer study, especially the whole question of the Caesarean text. To consider these it is necessary to observe what Streeter actually says, and for this purpose, not even a summary is adequate. The student must read and re-read pp. 3–148 in *The Four Gospels*.

[1] *Op. cit.*, 148.

XI

FURTHER DEVELOPMENTS SINCE STREETER

S TREETER's textual views have been presented at some length not only because of their interest and importance, but also because they both round off the theory of Westcott and Hort, and form a necessary starting-point for further developments. In both cases one of the most important causes of advance is the same, the discovery of new evidence—since Westcott and Hort the discovery of the Sinaitic Syriac, the Washington Codex, and Codex Koridethi[1]; and since Streeter the finding of new Papyrus manuscripts, especially the Chester Beatty Papyri and Papyrus Bodmer II—and in both cases also the patient and sustained study of investigators the world over. Textual Criticism never stands still. Every new discovery raises new problems and causes us to review accepted conclusions.

The study of present and possible future developments is naturally the field for advanced research, but it is advantageous even in an introductory work to survey the position already reached, the criticisms to which it is exposed, and the trend of existing discussions. This task will be attempted in the present chapter. The first step is to describe the reaction of scholars to Streeter's views.

After Streeter

Streeter's suggestions have won considerable support, especially in Great Britain, but interesting criticisms have

---

[1] See the important article of F. C. Burkitt, 'W and Θ: Studies in the Western Text of St. Mark,' *JTS*, xvii, 1–21, also his two later articles in the same journal, xxviii, 145, xxix, 1–16.

been evoked, in particular with regard to his claim for the existence and importance of the Caesarean family. First of all, however, some of his less striking suggestions may be considered.

His claim that MSS must be weighed, not counted, is entirely sound. Quite small groups like D k sy[s] may justly turn the scale in estimating the importance of readings, and nothing is gained by adding late MSS of no distinctive value. The need for a new thesaurus of various readings is manifestly great and the Byzantine text offers several real advantages as a foundation for this purpose, but it seems premature to cite MSS in groups until a wider consent about local texts has been gained, and small print and numbers and letters above the line are still needed for purposes of identification. Local texts still call for discussion; in particular the Caesarean family.

Local Texts

1. About most of these there is wide agreement. Few would dispute the view that the B ℵ text is a revision made early in the third century in Egypt and probably at Alexandria, although its attribution to Hesychius can be no more than a conjecture. Its high value is universally recognized, but not the almost exclusive status assigned to it by Westcott and Hort. Writing in 1913 A. Souter declared that, in his opinion, a great advance upon Westcott and Hort's text in the direction of the original autographs was highly improbable in his generation, but he recognized that much work remained to be done, especially as regards 'Western Non-Interpolations' in the light of the Old Syriac and its freedom from the interpolations characteristic of non-Western documents.[1] In the *Porter-Bacon Festschrift*, 21–47, in an article on the Text of the Gospels, Kirsopp Lake made a survey of the evidence in the major centres of Church life in the third century, and recognizing that the Western text was used everwhere wrote, 'I still think that

[1] *The Text and Canon of the New Testament*, 138–43.

the *neutral* text is intrinsically the better.'[1] Similar opinions can be quoted from many recent textual critics. The main point of present-day interest is the kind of text current in Egypt in the second century before the revision was made. It has been generally thought that this text was Western and that the line of development was from this to the B ℵ text, especially since Clement of Alexandria, in contrast with Origen, used a Western text. Streeter pointed out, however, that Clement came to Alexandria fairly late in life and had formerly lived in South Italy. He may then have brought a Western text of the Gospels with him when he migrated to Egypt, and in any case his quotations are usually from memory.[2] In this suggestion much is conjectural, but it is reasonable conjecture, and it warns us that too much may be made of the possibility that Clement found the Western text entrenched at Alexandria.

The text of P[66] has some bearing on this question. This Papyrus MS (Bodmer II) [3] may have come from Egypt and in the opinion of Professor Victor Martin[4] of Geneva and of other experts may have been written about A.D. 200. It may be premature to base much on its text which is being diligently studied. C. K. Barrett[5] writes, 'All we can say is that its readings were current at a very early date— perhaps within a century of the date when John was written. But even so, some of them may be erroneous.' An important article has recently been contributed to *New Testament Studies*[6] in which A. F. J. Klijn maintains that P[45] is much more Western than P[66]. The text of P[66] is mixed, but shows fewer Caesarean readings than P[45]. Klijn writes, 'We are

---

[1] *Op. cit.*, 45. [2] *The Four Gospels*, 57. [3] See earlier, p. 12.
[4] In *Papyrus Bodmer II: Évangile de Jean*, chaps. i–xiv (1956).
[5] *ET*, lxviii (March 1957), 174–7. Barrett, who is studying the text of P[66], examines the readings of this MS in 18 passages in Jn. i–xiv which involve well-known and important textual problems. For readings in Jn. xiv–xxi, supplied by Professor V. Martin of Geneva, see the 2nd ed. of the British and Foreign Bible Society's Edition of the Nestle text. [6] Vol. 3 (July 1957), 327–34.

F

dealing here with a text which, as compared with P⁴⁵, is more in agreement with B ℵ. This is important as we have here a text which is about fifty years older. This means that P⁶⁶ goes against the tradition from Western to B ℵ. It is therefore unwise to speak about a gradual development in the direction of B ℵ. It is much safer to say that we have a number of traditions in Egypt.'[1] It will be interesting to see how far this judgement is confirmed by other investigators. Meantime it would seem that we are obtaining glimpses of B ℵ readings which are much older than the third century revision.

2. As regards the *Western Text*, in the geographical sense of the word, and its two sub-divisions, African (k e Cyprian) and European (D a b Irenaeus), considerable agreement has been reached, the main problems being the omissions of D in the Gospels and its additions in the Acts. Above all, the origin of this text remains a constant and almost baffling issue.

The hypothesis of F. Blass,[2] that Luke wrote the Gospel and the Acts in two editions, represented by the Alexandrian text in the earlier edition of the Gospel and the later of Acts, and by the Western text in the later edition of the Gospel and the earlier of Acts, has not commended itself to scholars in general and is rejected by most of them. The suggestion that the Greek text of the Acts in D has been strongly influenced by the Latin,[3] or alternatively by the Old Syriac,[4] has also failed to command wide assent.[5] The same must be said also of the attempt of A. C. Clark[6] to show that the differences between the δ and β texts are due to scribal errors and, in the Acts, to the desire for abbreviation. Clark's

---

[1] *Op. cit.*, 331.   [2] See *The Philology of the Gospels* (1898).

[3] Cf. J. Rendel Harris, *A Study of Codex Bezae* (1891).

[4] Cf. F. H. Chase, *The Old Syriac Element in the Text of Codex Bezae* (1893), *The Syro-Latin Text of the Gospels* (1895).

[5] Cf. F. G. Kenyon, *The Text of the Greek Bible*, 94f.

[6] *The Primitive Text of the Gospels and Acts* (1914), *The Acts of the Apostles* (1933).

ingenious hypothesis is examined in detail by F. G. Kenyon in an important pamphlet entitled 'The Western Text in the Gospels and Acts',[1] and his conclusions have great force. 'It would appear,' he writes, 'that North Africa was the home of the δ text, that it spread (with modifications) to Italy, and that some copies of it found their way to Egypt and elsewhere in the East. But that it was ever dominant in the East does not seem to be proved, and the improbability of the Western text being superior to the Eastern remains to be taken into account.'[2] The opinion of J. H. Ropes,[3] that the δ text is a second-century revision in connexion with an early stage in the formation of the Canon, has been widely commended. In default of a better explanation we must ascribe the differences to scribal or, more probably, editorial activity, with the recognition that many of the Western additions in the Acts are the work of a writer with considerable knowledge of early tradition, and the opinion that most of the omissions in the Gospels, though not all, represent the original text.[4]

In recent years attention has been drawn to the Aramaic element in the Western Text. Wellhausen called attention to this element in the Bezan text in the first edition of his *Einleitung in die drei ersten Evangelien* (1905). J. H. Moulton[5] observed that, if this Aramaic basis is proved, we have manifestly taken a big step towards the solution of our great textual question, and W. F. Howard[6] contributed an

---

[1] *Proceedings of the British Academy* (1940). [2] *Op. cit.*, 30.
[3] *The Beginnings of Christianity*, part I, vol. III.
[4] Cf. C. S. C. Williams, *The Acts of the Apostles*, 30f, F. F. Bruce, *The Acts of the Apostles*, 43f, F. G. Kenyon, *op. cit.*, 26f.
[5] *Prolegomena*, 242.
[6] As regards Mark, Howard endorses the opinion of Lagrange, 'His Greek is always Greek, yet translation Greek; not that he translates an Aramaic writing, but because he reproduces an Aramaic κατήχησις.' In Lk. i, ii and Acts Howard prefers to explain the Semitisms by the influence of the Septuagint on Luke's style. So N. Turner, *NTS*, ii, 100–9 in reply to P. Winter, *NTS* i, 111–21 with reference to Lk. i, ii.

invaluable Appendix on 'Semitisms in the New Testament' in vol. II of Moulton's *Grammar* (1929). C. C. Torrey has long maintained that behind the Gospels and Acts i–xv there was an Aramaic original. In *Documents of the Primitive Church* (1941) he put forward the hypothesis that at the end of the first century the Gospels and Acts were translated into an Aramaic Targum and that a retranslation of this into Greek was the basis of the δ text. M. Black commends the unpublished work of the late A. J. Wensinck of Leiden who claims that D represents the Aramaic background of the Synoptic tradition more faithfully than do the non-Western MSS. Black himself suggests that, while the differences between D and B ℵ do not point to the existence of two editions of the Gospels, they do suggest two (or more) redactions of what was substantially, if not verbally, the same original Gospel text, and that 'the Bezan redaction' has left more of the 'Aramaized' Greek text in an unrevised form than the redaction represented by B ℵ.[1] These suggestions will be debated for many years to come. They are mentioned here to illustrate directions in which the study of the Western text is moving.

3. The *Eastern Text* presents difficulties of its own, but its existence in the two familes, Antiochian (sy[s] and sy[c]) and Caesarean (Θ and its allies), is generally admitted, with hesitations and suggested modifications in the case of the Caesarean text. During a long period the Eastern Text of Syria was included in the 'Western' Text. It certainly agrees frequently with the δ text, but as F. C. Burkitt[2] has shown this affinity may be due to the influence of Tatian's *Diatessaron*. The continued study of the Sinaitic Syriac, unknown to Westcott and Hort, has revealed closer affinities with the β text, and has led to the belief that sy[s] and sy[c] were based on a distinctive form of the Greek text current in Antioch. If only Greek MSS containing this text had

---

[1] *An Aramaic Approach to the Gospels and Acts* (1946, 2nd ed. 1954), 214.

[2] *Evangelion da-Mepharreshe* (1904).

survived and the Greek text of the *Diatessaron* were extant, these conjectures might be expected to receive further support. Meantime the authorities for the Antiochian text are the two Old Syriac MSS, sy[s] and sy[c], supported by non-Byzantine and non-Western readings in the later Syriac versions (sy[p], sy[h], sy[pal]) and the Armenian.

Streeter's opinions regarding the *Caesarean Text* have been, and still remain, the subject of lively debate. In a review of *The Four Gospels* Burkitt wrote, 'My chief objection to speaking of "the Caesarean text" is that this term gives apparent definiteness and consistence to a set of "various readings" that remain to me obstinately disparate and amorphous.'[1] To this criticism Streeter replied that when speaking of 'the Caesarean text' he meant the majority of the readings which are either peculiar to, or only rarely found outside, this group of authorities. Burkitt added a note objecting to the sub-division of the Eastern group of witnesses into the Antiochian and Caesarean families.[2] On the other side F. G. Kenyon observed that 'we have now in the Caesarean family, whatever its origin and character, a well-established entity, comparable in date with the Neutral group, and with no extravagances to arouse suspicions'.[3]

Since Streeter wrote in 1924 modifications of his Caesarean hypothesis have been suggested. After a close examination of the relevant evidence K. Lake, R. P. Blake, and S. New suggested[4] that Origen used a 'Caesarean' text at Alexandria, an Alexandrian text after his departure to Caesarea in A.D. 231, and then later at Caesarea a Caesarean text. In the closing pages of the sixth edition of *The Text of the New Testament*[5] Lake and Mrs. New agree that the text of Θ and its allies is the local text of Caesarea, but they believe it to be 'merely a correction of the Western by the Neutral'

---

[1] *JTS*, 26 (1924–25), 278–94.   [2] *JTS*, 26 (1924–25), 373–80.
[3] *Recent Developments*, 70f.
[4] 'The Caesarean Text of the Gospel of Mark', *HTR*, xxi (1928), 207–404.   [5] Twelfth Impression, 84f.

rather than an independent text co-ordinate in value with these texts; it is 'a mixed text' which presupposes the existence of the β text, which is not the invention of Origen, but is anterior to him.[1]   Later, in 1935, T. Ayuso published a thorough analysis of the evidence in the light of P[45] and suggested that the 'Caesarean' text was carried to Caesarea from Egypt where it originated in a locality off the beaten track so far as scholarship was concerned, in the region of Gizeh and the Fayyum.[2]   He distinguished a pre-Caesarean text represented by P[45] W (in part) fam. 1 28 and fam. 13 and a Caesarean text proper found in Θ. 565 and 700.

In a valuable comment on these discussions C. S. C. Williams thinks that for the present it may be well to regard the members of the Caesarean group as those of a *clan* rather than of a *family* which had its origin in Egypt and was popularized in Caesarea.[3]   He goes so far as to say that any hopes based on Streeter's work that here we should find a pre-Byzantine textual type independent of and as valuable as the 'Western' and the Alexandrian 'seem now very remote'.

It will be seen that the character and origin of the Caesarean group is still very much under discussion.   It may well be that the reaction against Streeter's views has gone too far.   At any rate, three considerations need to be borne in mind: (1) As regards P[45] it must be remembered that a MS is not always an authority for the text current in the locality where it is discovered (e.g. Θ); (2) At various times MSS have been removed from the place of origin to different regions (e.g. W); (3) Origen, a scholarly textual critic, may have sought MSS from other centres in addition to those of Alexandria and Egypt.   After all, Caesarea is little more than three hundred miles by sea from Alexandria and Origen had relationships with it long before he finally settled there in A.D. 231.   We know that he lived there A.D. 215-19.

---

[1] *Op.cit.*, 85.   [2] *Biblica*, xvi (1935), 369-415.

[3] A. H. M'Neile, *Introduction to the New Testament* (ed. C. S. Williams), 389.

What was to prevent him from acquiring Caesarean MSS either then or later? His commentary on John suggests that for a time he hesitated in the use of the Caesarean text before deciding definitely to use MSS of this kind when he became resident in Palestine. These considerations are speculative and we are far from being able to demonstrate their validity; but they are not irrelevant. At present it is perhaps too soon to speak of the 'so-called' Caesarean text or to think of it as a clan rather than a family. In a sense all families are clans, since like emigrants members of them may in the course of time wander far from their original habitat.

4. The *Byzantine Text*, or Textus Receptus, gains a new interest if families additional to the Alexandrian and the Western are recognized. In this situation the Byzantine text is more inclusive than a combination of the β and δ texts. In addition to the use of these families its editors must have drawn upon Antiochian and Caesarean MSS, since presumably these are of earlier origin. In fact, P[45] contains Byzantine readings which are earlier than *c.* A.D. 250, that is, before the Byzantine text was compiled.[1] In short, this text is more eclectic than we had supposed.

Here is a field for study which calls for further investigation. Nothing but good can come from the closer study of Greek MSS, early versions, and Patristic texts which is being steadily pursued in Great Britain, America, and Germany by the American Bible Society in consultation with the National Bible Society of Scotland, and the Württembergische Bibelanstalt in Stuttgart.[2]

[1] See examples in the list of readings from P[45] printed in my commentary on Mark, p. 41f.

[2] See *NTS*, iv, 344f. In this article M. Black writes, ' It is plainly too early to forecast the shape of the text to come: but the number of passages where the committee judgement requires a change in the WH text is impressive.' Further, a group of American and British scholars have formed an International Committee in order to assemble and publish an extensive *apparatus criticus*. See *NTS*, ii, 222f, and *The Proceedings of the British Academy*, vol. xl (1954) onwards.

XII
NOTES ON SELECT READINGS

As INDICATED in the Preface this chapter contains notes on Select Readings, thirty-four in number, supplied with explanatory observations. The purpose of the selection is to give guidance in the interpretation of the manuscript tradition and to show how textual principles are applied by experts and commentators. It must be emphasized at the outset that the passages chosen for comment are not representative of New Testament readings in general, for there can be little doubt in most cases how the text should be read. They illustrate doctrinal, historical, and harmonistic modifications, together with glosses, emendations, and conjectures, in order, if possible, to show how such matters should be judged.

It is arguable that the facts should be presented without comment so that the reader may form his own conclusions, but it has seemed to the writer a better plan to give a personal opinion when one is held. These opinions, however, are not to be regarded as solutions, but as judgements open to challenge, the only necessary condition being that, where the reader takes a different view, he should be able to sustain it by sound arguments based on the manuscript tradition and the use of recognized textual principles. In this way alone, I believe, he will best discover for himself the importance and fascination of textual criticism. The select readings may, of course, be studied by individual readers, but a better plan is to examine them in a group or seminar guided by a tutor.

The notation described in Chapter II is used in the readings

and other necessary information is given in the footnotes.
A few symbols additional to those listed on p. 5f include
the following:

An asterisk (*) after a MS indicates that the original reading is meant.

The sign 'pt' (e.g. arm^{pt}) means that only partial support
is given. Alternatively, brackets mean the same.

habent 'have' precedes MSS which give the reading.

it   the Old Latin Version.

mg   a marginal reading.

om   omit.

omn   all MSS (uncials or minuscules).

R^t   the text of the Revised Version.

R^m   the margin of the Revised Version.

RSV   the American Revised Standard Version.

vid   *videtur*, apparently, or an uncertain reading.

In the footnotes to the various readings the MSS described
in Chapters III–VI and the Patristic writers mentioned in
Chapter VII are assumed to be known, but other MSS,
except minuscules, and signs are explained. Abbreviations
which indicate the number of MSS in question (*pc, al, pm,
pl, rell*) were explained on p. 6. Other signs of the same
kind are:

pler =many others.

plur =most others.

After a square bracket (]) variant readings follow separated
by colons (:) or vertical strokes (|).

Well-known commentaries and some of the works already
frequently mentioned are referred to simply by the page.

As is usual in textual notes the Greek is quoted without
accents.

c =circa, 'about'; *cum* = 'with'; *apud* = 'in the writings
of'.

1. *Mt. i. 16*

Ιακωβ δε εγεννησεν τον Ιωσηφ τον ανδρα Μαριας εξ ης εγγενηθη Ιησους ο λεγομενος χριστος P¹ unc. *plur.* min. *plur.* syᴾ ʰ ᵖᵃˡ geo arm aeth Tert Aug: Ιακωβ δε εγεννησεν τον Ιωσηφ ω μνηστευθεισα παρθενος Μαριαμ εγεννησεν Ιησουν τον λεγομενον χριστον Θ fam. 13 a b c d g¹ (k) (q) syᶜ arm: Ιακωβ δε εγεννησεν τον Ιωσηφ. Ιωσηφ [δε] ω μνηστευθεισα ην παρθενος Μαριαμ εγεννησεν Ιησουν τον λεγομενον χριστον syˢ.

This passage is of great interest because in some respects doctrinal modifications have affected the text. The second reading, which is mainly Caesarean and Western, omits τον ανδρα Μαριας and sharpens the allusion to the Virgin Birth by means of the phrase μνηστευθεισα παρθενος Μαριαμ, leaving the subject of εγεννησεν uncertain or at least ambiguous. This ambiguity is resolved in the third reading, in which Ιωσηφ is the subject of εγεννησεν. A similar reading has been attributed to the *Dialogue of Timothy and Aquila*, where the first reading quoted above is followed by the words, 'And Joseph begat Jesus who is called Christ', but this passage is probably the inference of the Jew, not part of the quotation (So Burkitt, *Evan. da-Meph.*, ii, 265).

In considering the textual problem it is essential to observe the nature of the Matthaean Genealogy. Obviously artificial in structure, its purpose is to affirm the Davidic descent of Jesus by tracing the royal line, and the verb εγεννησεν is used throughout of legal, not physical descent. The same is also true of the reading of syˢ, for in the parenthesis, 'to whom was betrothed Mary the Virgin', it manifestly presupposes the doctrine of the Virgin Birth.

Most editors and commentators accept the first reading which, as will be seen, is widely and strongly attested. Apparently the phrase τον ανδρα Μαριας gave offence to later scribes who modified the passage as indicated in the alternative readings. A few scholars have suggested that even the first reading has undergone modification, since, in contrast to the rest of the Genealogy, εγεννηθη in the last link of the chain is used of physical parentage. They think that the Evangelist would have continued to use εγεννησεν in the same legal sense to the end and conjecture that the original reading may have been, 'And Jacob begat Joseph, the husband of Mary. And Joseph begat Jesus who is called Christ.' See my discussion in *The Historical Evidence for the Virgin Birth*, 104-14. But this conjecture has no textual support, apart from the fact that each phrase in it is attested in the textual tradition. The opinion is preferred that εγεννηθη is the result of the Evangelist's intention to adjust the Virgin Birth tradition to the fact of the Messianic descent. This view may well be sound, but is not altogether easy to accept by any one who has reflected upon the peculiar character of the Genealogy and the later modifications in the textual tradition.

Notes. P[1] contains Mt. i. (iii–iv). c Colbertinus (xii). g[1] Sangermanensis I (viii–ix).

2. Mt. xvi. 2f

οψιας γενομενης . . . δυνασθε C D L W Θ fam. 1 22 33 it sy[d] p h bo Eus: Om. ℵ B X Y Γ 047 fam. 13 157 sy[s] c arm Or.

This passage is clearly an addition to the text of Mt. as its omission by the texts of Alexandria and Antioch, by some of the authorities of the Caesarean text, and by Origen indicates. But it is not due to a harmonization with Lk. xii. 54-6, to which it has a marked resemblance, for its linguistic agreement with this passage is slight. Streeter, 241f, suggests that the Matthaean text has been drawn from a tradition independent of Lk. and inserted at an early date in the Western text. So also Westcott and Hort, *Notes* 13.

Notes. X Monacensis (x). Y Macedonianus (ix). Γ Tischendorfianus IV (ix–x). 047 Andreensis (x).

3. Mt. xxiv. 36

ουδε ο υιος ℵ* B D Θ Φ *et al.* fam. 13 (except 69) 28 *et al.* it *pler.* vg (4) sy[pal] arm geo[1] *et* 2B aeth Tat Iren Or Chr

Ambr *codd. latini apud* Jer: Om. ℵ^{ca} L W Δ Σ fam. 1 33
565 700 *et al* g^{1.2} l r² vg *pler.* sy^{s p h} bo sa geo²ᴬ *codd. graeci
apud* Jer *et* Ambr.

This textual problem is very difficult to decide as the
differing opinions of commentators show. See the references
in Taylor, *Mk.*, 522. There can be no question of the genuineness of the saying. Cf. Schmiedel, *EB*, ii, col. 1881. The
point at issue is whether Matthew omitted the phrase which
implies a limitation in the Son's knowledge of the time of the
Parousia, or whether scribes omitted it from reverential
motives. The reading caused great embarrassment during
the time of the Arian controversy.

The textual evidence strongly supports the originality
of the phrase in Mt. It is attested by the leading representatives of the Alexandrian, Western, and Caesarean families
and by Patristic quotations from the second century on-
wards. But it is omitted in most Syriac MSS (sy^{s p h}, sy^c
is defective here), that is to say, in MSS from the region in
which Matthew was probably written and where, if Streeter's
principle (see p. 64) is right, we should expect an accidental
omission to be corrected (but see Streeter, 135), and it is
also omitted by important MSS belonging to the families
mentioned above. The case is one in which the critic's
judgement is likely to oscillate. Elsewhere Matthew omits
questions asked by Jesus which might seem to imply want
of knowledge on His part (cf. M'Neile, 113), and for the
reader's consideration it may be suggested that *ουδε ο υιος*
was wanting in the original text of Mt. xxiv. 36 and by
assimilation to the text of Mk. xiii. 32 was added in most
textual families at a very early date. See further Taylor,
Mk., 522, and for the opposite view C. S. C. Williams, 38.
See also the discussions in Westcott and Hort, *Notes*, 17f
and Streeter, 135, 594.

Notes. g² Sangermanensis II (x–xi). l Rehdigeranus (vii).
r² Usserianus II (vii). Ambr = Ambrose 397. Jer = Jerome 420
Tat = Tatian *c.* 170. *codd. graeci apud* Jer *et* Ambr = Greek codices

as quoted by Jerome and Ambrose. The figure after a version indicates the number of MSS with the reading.

4. *Mt. xxvii. 16f*

βαραββαν] *Ιησουν Βαραββαν* Θ fam. 1 209 241 299 sy[s] [pal] arm geo[2] Or.

This addition is a remarkable example of a name found only in a comparatively small number of MSS which has been accepted in recent years by many scholars as genuine. This fact is not surprising since it is attested by the principal members of two families, by Θ fam. 1, and sy[s]. Origen strongly disliked the reading and regarded it as a heretical interpolation, but it stood in the text of Matthew on which he was commenting. It was absent, he declared, from many MSS. Both intrinsic and transcriptional probability favour the reading, for it is not likely that a scribe would add the name 'Jesus' to Barabbas, but quite probable that he would be inclined to omit the name. Streeter suggested that the name in the abbreviated form may have been omitted by the common error of haplography if the text read $\overline{\text{YMININ}}$, and once omitted preference would be given to the shorter text. It has also been suggested that *Ιησους* originally stood in Mk. xv. 7 before the words *ο λεγομενος Βαραββας* but this, of course, is conjectural. Deissmann, who drew attention to the reading in Mt. xxvii. 16f in his essay 'The Name "Jesus" ' in *Mysterium Christi* (1930), wrote, 'This text, just because it was later felt to be an inbearable scandal and was altered, mocks every hypothesis of the unhistoricity of Jesus of Nazareth' (p. 21). He adds, 'This piece of original text should be confidently restored to its place in modern revisions of the Bible — even though the simple Bible reader with his pious aversion from the text may still feel difficulties' (*ibid.*). See further Deissmann, *op. cit.*, 3–27, Streeter, 87, 95, 101, 136, and C. S. C. Williams, 31–3. See also for its interest Westcott and Hort's long discussion, *Notes*, 19f. They wrote, it must be remembered, before Θ and sy[s] were known. It is interesting to note that translators who apparently accept the reading hesitate to introduce it into the text.

5. *Mk. i. 1*

υιου Θεου] א[a] B D L W it vg sy[p h] sa bo geo[2] arm (3) Iren Or[lat] Aug (υι. τ. θ., A fam. 1 fam. 13 565 700 R[t]): Om. א* Θ 28 sy[pal] geo[1] arm[pt] Iren Or Bas Vict Jer[pt].

Commentators are widely divided on the question whether υιου Θεου should be read. The reading is strongly supported by Alexandrian (א[a] B L) and Western (D it vg) authorities and by important Caesarean MSS (fam. 1 fam. 13 565 700). The families, however, are divided. א* omits the phrase, but is corrected in א[a]. Θ also favours the omission, but is in contrast with its usual allies (except 28). The versions and the Fathers can be quoted on both sides.

The problem is obviously difficult to resolve. Westcott and Hort omit the reading from their text, but say that 'neither reading can be safely rejected', *Notes*, 23. Both the RV and the RSV have 'the Son of God' in their texts, but record the omission in their margins. For the Patristic evidence see C. H. Turner, *JTS*, xxviii. 150.

It is possible that both readings may have appeared from the beginning, the full text as a title and the shorter text in the opening words of the Gospel, or at an early stage υιου Θεου may have been omitted by homoioteleuton. The doctrine that Jesus is the Son of God is fully in harmony with Mark's Christology (see Taylor, *Mk.*, 152) and on the whole the procedure adopted by the Revisers seems the best.

Notes. Bas =Basil of Caesarea 397. Vict =Victor 304.

6. *Mk. i. 41*

σπλαχνισθεις] οργισθεις D a d ff[2] r[1]

This is a case in which the Western authorities stand alone against the rest of the textual authorities. Westcott and

Hort suggest that οργισθεις may have been suggested by
v. 43 or is perhaps derived from an extraneous source, *Notes*,
23. This explanation is hardly satisfactory, for it is easy to
see why 'being angry' may have been changed to 'being full
of compassion', but not easy to account for the alteration
vice versa. This explanation has been widely accepted (see
Taylor, *Mk.*, 187).

Notes. ff.² Corbeiensis II (v–vi). r¹ Usserianus I (vii)

7. *Mk. vi. 3*

ουχ ουτος εστιν ο τεκτων, ο υιος της Μαριας;] Unc *omn.*
fam. 1 28 892 1071 *al. pler.* f ff² l q vg *pler* syᵖ ʰ sa bo geo¹:
ο του τεκτονος υιος P⁴⁵ fam. 13 33 565 579 700 a b c e i r²
aur. vg *plur* bo (3) aeth (Most, except P⁴⁵, add either και
της Μαριας, και Μαριας, or Μαριας)

On the basis of the textual evidence it is not easy to decide
which of the two readings should be accepted. The first
reading implies a knowledge of the Virgin Birth tradition
which otherwise is not present in Mk. It is represented in all
branches of the textual tradition, strongly, though not
exclusively, in the Alexandrian text (א B *al* 892 sa bo),
in the Caesarean (Θ fam. 1 28 1071 geo¹), in the Western
(D f ff² l q vg) (but apparently not in the African Latin), and
in the later Antiochian text (syᵖ ʰ). But, on the other hand, the
reading ο του τεκτονος υιος is found in some representatives
of the Alexandrian text (33 579 boᵖᵗ), notably in the Caesarean (P⁴⁵ fam. 13 565 700, but not in Θ), in the European
Latin (a b c i r²), the vg *plur.* and the African Latin (e).

The balance tilts in the direction of ο τεκτων, but other
considerations render this conclusion uncertain. Origen,
Contra Celsum, vi. 36, denies that Jesus is anywhere described
as an artizan in the Gospels, and Hort's explanation, *Notes*,
24, that Origen forgot Mk. vi. 3 or did not hold Mark responsible for the words of the Galileans, is hardly satisfactory.
Further, neither Matthew nor Luke support ο τεκτων.

Mt. xiii. 55 reads ουχ ουτος εστιν ο του τεκτονος υιος; ουχ η μητηρ αυτου λεγεται Μαριαμ ... ; and Lk. iv. 22 (non-Marcan) has ουχι υιος εστιν Ιωσηφ ουτος; Moreover, the phrase ο υιος της Μαριας in Mk. raises difficulties, since it is contrary to Jewish custom to describe a man as the son of his mother, except in terms of contempt (cf. Judg. xi. 1f). 'On the evidence as a whole it seems best to conclude that Mark wrote ο του τεκτονος υιος and that an early scribe replaced this reading by ο τεκτων and added ο υιος της Μαριας'. Cf. Taylor, *Mk.*, 300. The alternative is to suggest that the variant reading may be an assimilation to Mt. xiii. 55 in order to rebut the idea that Jesus was ever engaged in a menial occupation. Cf. C. S. C. Williams, 30.

Notes. i Vindobonensis (v–vi). aur Aureus (viii).

8. *Mk. viii. 26*

Μηδε εις την κωμην εισελθης μηδε ειπης τινι εν τη κωμη A C Δ E G *et al.* 118 33 579 700 892 1071 sy[p h] aeth goth: μηδε (μη ℵ* W) εις την κωμην εισελθης ℵ* B L W fam. 1 (except 118) sy[s] sa bo geo[1]: μηδενι ειπης εις την κωμην D c q k: μηδενι ειπης μηδε (μηδε om Θ Φ 565) εν τη κωμη (εν τη κωμη om it (except ff[2]) vg) Θ Φ fam. 13 (except 124) 28 61 565 it vg.

The first passage (the TR) is one of the eight conflate readings on which Westcott and Hort (99f) base their claim for the superiority of the 'Neutral' text. They classed this reading as 'Syrian', the second as 'Neutral' and the third as 'Western', and naturally preferred the 'Neutral'. That the first reading is a conflation of the second and third is undoubted, but in view of the increased evidence now available it is open to question whether priority should be given to the reading μηδε εις την κωμην εισελθης. It is true that the additional MSS, fam. 1 and sy[s], can now be cited for it, but the authority of the Western text is greatly increased by the similar reading in the Caesarean MSS Θ fam. 13 28 and 565 (the fourth reading above), apart from the dative εν τη κωμη. In the light of Marcan usage Turner strongly supports εις c.acc. as in D and many Old Latin MSS.

There is therefore much to be said for μηδενι ειπης εις την κωμην, especially for the injunction in this reading to keep silence regarding the cure, which is a characteristic feature of Mark's Gospel (the Messianic Secret). See Taylor, *Mk.*, 373. It may also be claimed that a charge to tell no man of the cure is intrinsically more probable than a bare command not to enter the village.

Notes. Δ Sangallensis (ix–x). E Basiliensis (viii). G Wolfi A (ix–x).

9. *Mk. ix. 41*

εν ονοματι οτι Χριστου εστε] ονοματι ℵc A B C* L 1 579 892 *al* sy[s] [p] [h] arm; R[m]: ον. μου ℵ* C³ W 118 124: τω ονοματι μου D Δ Θ fam. 13 (except 124) 28 565 700 it vg sy[h] [mg] sa bo aeth Or: Χρ. εστε] εμον εστε ℵ*

This reading is of much interest because it raises the possibility of an interesting conjecture. It is widely agreed that χριστου is the addition of an editor (Hawkins, *Horae Synopticae* 152) or a copyist (Lagrange, 249). If so, it must have been a very early attempt to remove a difficulty in the original text. At first sight the reading ονοματι μου, with or without εν and the definite article, appears to be original. But these readings are probably too easy. Why should 'in my name' call for alteration? A reading seems to be presumed which was obscure and needed explanation. Moreover, the parallel in Mt. x. 42 reads εις ονομα μαθητου, and this suggests that the offering of water is the *characteristic act* of a disciple, not only an act in Christ's name. Further, the readings with μου, while strongly attested, belong mainly to the Western (D W it vg) and Caesarean (Θ fam. 13 565 700) groups with 28, the later versions and Origen, and are omitted by a powerful Alexandrian group (B C* L 579 892) supported by sy[s] [p] [h] arm. In these circumstances εμον in ℵ* is worthy of note.

G

In a letter T. W. Manson pointed out to me that the obvious correction is εμοι and that εν ονοματι οτι εμοι εστε would give a perfectly good sense and account for Matthew's interpretation ('on the ground that you are mine', cf. τους εμους in viii. 38). One will naturally hesitate to accept a conjecture based on the incorrect text of a single MS, but it will be difficult to suggest a better explanation of this textual problem (cf. Taylor, *Mk.*, 408).

Notes. C², the reading of a corrector of C.

10. *Mk. x. 2*

προσελθοντες Φαρισαιοι] Om. D a b k sy⁸

Although the number of MSS which omit this phrase is small, their combined testimony is very strong since they are the principal representatives of three families, those of Italy and Gaul (D a b), Carthage (k), and Antioch (sy⁸). It is not surprising that the omission is accepted by many scholars, including Wellhausen, 78, Burkitt, 98, Turner, 47, *JTS*, xxix, 5. The MSS are supported by intrinsic probability, for no good reason can be given for the omission of the reference to the Pharisees, while it would not be strange for an allusion to the well-known opponents of Jesus to be supplied if the verb lacked a subject. Moreover, if the phrase is not original, the verb επηρωτων is an impersonal plural, 'People were asking him', a construction of which there are many examples in Mk. (cf. Taylor, *Mk.*, 47f). For these reasons the reading προσελθοντες Φαρισαιοι should probably be rejected.

11. *Mk. x. 12*

και εαν αυτη απολυσασα τον ανδρα αυτης γαμηση αλλον ℵ B C L Δ Ψ 579 892 1342 sa bo aeth: εαν γυνη απολυση τον ανδρα αυτης και γαμηθη αλλω A N X Y Π Σ Φ 22 118 1071 *al pler* f g² r² vg syᵖ ʰ Aug (εαν απολ. γ. W fam. 1 geo¹): γυνη εαν (εαν γ. D) εξελθη απο (του) ανδρος και γαμηση αλλον (γαμηθη αλλω) D (Θ) fam. 13 28 543 565 700 a b ff² (k) q arm sy⁸

This passage is of much interest for historical as well as textual reasons.

The first reading is well attested, but almost exclusively by Alexandrian authorities. In the second the evidence is more widely distributed, but is not impressive. The third reading is widely represented by MSS representative of all the great families (the texts of Antioch, Caesarea, Carthage, and Italy and Gaul) except the text of Alexandria. It is at least as early as *c.* A.D. 150 and may be much earlier. Wellhausen, 78, says *Nur so kann Mc geschrieben haben.*

In defending the third reading F. C. Burkitt suggests that Jesus is referring to the well-known case of Herodias and claims that the saying is 'one of the really primitive features of the Gospel of Mark', *The Gospel History and its Transmission*, 99–101.

The statements in the first two readings are contrary to Jewish law according to which a woman cannot divorce her husband. Even the third reading, although more Jewish in character, is exposed to the same criticism, since apparently the women marries a second husband while the first is still alive. In the form in which it appears in the first two settings the saying has been adapted to the conditions of the Gentile world. The third form is intelligible if Burkitt's suggestion is accepted. It is less likely that a copyist has given it a more Jewish formulation, since the adaptation, if made, is only partial. See Taylor, *Mk.*, 420f.

Notes. Π Petropolitanus II (ix).

12. Mk. xii. 23

εν τη αναστασει ℵ B C D L W Δ Ψ 33 579 892 c d k r¹ syᵖ sa bo *pler*: +οταν αναστωσιν A X Γ Θ Π Σ Φ *et al* fam. 1 (fam. 13) 565 700 1071 a b ff² i q vg syˢ ʰ arm geo bo (1 MS).

This example is chosen because it illustrates the way in which stylistic considerations affect textual problems. The question at issue is whether the redundant οταν αναστωσιν should be read. The textual evidence on both sides is rather evenly balanced, for, while the MSS which omit the phrase are strongly Alexandrian and those which read it are Caesarean and Antiochian (note sy[s]), the Western testimony is divided.　In these circumstances the fact that redundancy is a feature of Mark's style and reflects Semitic idiom (cf. xiii. 19f) suggests that the addition should be read. Such considerations ought not to be allowed to discount the importance of the manuscript tradition.　Nor can intrinsic and transcriptional probability be neglected.　Indeed when a phrase otherwise strongly attested is omitted by the text of Alexandria the question arises whether the omission may not be due to deliberate editing in the interests of style.　This possibility cannot be exalted into a principle but it should never be ignored.　A similar example presents itself in the next reading.

13. *Mk. xiv. 25*

ουκετι ου μη (πιω) A B Δ *et al.* min. *pler.* b ff² i l q r² vg sy[s] [p] [h] sa geo (arm): ου μη πιω ℵ C (D) L W 471 892 1342 (a) c (f) k vg (1 MS) bo aeth: ου μη προσθω(-ωμεν Θ) πιειν (πειν D) D (Θ) 565 a f arm.

A clear Semitism is present in the third reading in D (cf. the use of the Hiphil of *yāsăph* 'to add' *c.* infin. in the LXX). Cf. Lk. xx. 11f.　This reading appears to be interpreted in the first reading and misunderstood in the second.　Literally rendered the third reading is 'I will not add to drink' = 'I will not drink again'.

14. *Mk. xiv. 62*

Εγω ειμι] συ ειπας οτι εγω ειμι Θ fam. 13 472 543 565 700 1071 geo arm Or.

This reading is included because of its considerable historical interest.　The familiar reading Εγω ειμι is generally accepted by editors and commentators in preference to the Caesarean alternative as a direct claim on the part of Jesus to be the Messiah.　It should be noted that the alternative text is also affirmative, but it expresses a difference of interpretation, 'The word is yours', 'Yes, if you like', indicating that the Speaker has His own ideas about Messiahship which are very different from those of the priests. Origen attests it in his commentary on Jn.

On purely textual grounds it would be hazardous to accept the Caesarean variant in the face of the witness of all other families in favour of the direct reply, 'I am', but several considerations may be urged in its support. Mt. xxvi. 64 has συ ειπας and Lk. xxii. 70 υμεις λεγετε οτι εγω ειμι, and these readings can more readily be accounted for if the Marcan variant is original. Further, the latter preserves the note of reserve regarding Messiahship so frequently found in Mk. The reading is accepted by Streeter, 322, and is commended by Lohmeyer, *Mk.*, 328*n*. Alternatively, the reading may be explained as the gloss of a copyist based on Mt. xxvi. 64, that is, as an example of assimilation, but for the reasons given it is not easy to accept this explanation. Probably the variant deserves more favourable consideration than it has yet received.

15. *Mk. xvi. 9–20*

(The Longer Ending) A C D L W Θ *et plur.* min. *plur.* it (except k) vg sy$^{(c)}$ p sa *pler.* bo arm (1 MS, E 229, *Presbyter Ariston*) aeth. Tat Iren Just: *Om* ℵ B k sy^s arm (8) geo^1 ^{et} ^{2A} aeth (3) Eus: (The Shorter Ending) 'But all that had been commanded them they announced briefly to those who were with Peter; (and) after this Jesus Himself appeared and from the East as far as the West He sent through them the holy and incorruptible proclamation of eternal salvation.' L Ψ 099 0112 274^{mg} 579 k sy$^{h\ mg}$ bo^{pt}: (The Freer Logion) 'And they made their defence saying This age of lawlessness and unbelief is under Satan who by unclean spirits does not allow the true power of God to be apprehended: wherefore reveal thy righteousness now' (So Jerome). 'They were speaking to Christ and Christ made the reply to them that the limit of the years of Satan's power is fulfilled but other terrible things draw near and on behalf of these sinners I was delivered up to death, that they might turn to the truth and sin no more, in order that they may inherit the spiritual and immortal glory of righteousnes, that is in heaven.' W *post* verse 14.

The evidence is decisively against the three endings given above. Although widely attested the Longer Ending is omitted by the principal members of the Alexandrian (ℵ B), the African Latin (k), and the Antiochian (sy^s) families, supported by the ancient versions and Eusebius. The Shorter Ending is even less well attested.[1] L and Ψ have both readings and so bring doubt upon each, while 099 and 0112 are late uncial fragments of the seventh century. The style and diction of the two readings tell strongly against their originality, since they contain words, phrases, and constructions not otherwise found in Mk. This is true also of the Freer Logion which appears after verse 14 only in W. In all three cases the subject-matter is manifestly that of a later period.

Patristic testimony (Tatian, Irenaeus, Justin Martyr) shows that the Longer Ending was added at an early date. From the evidence as a whole the only conclusion we can draw is that either Mk. ended originally at xvi. 8 or, what is far more probable, that the original ending was lost almost at once by some mischance, probably from the autograph itself.

For important discussions see Westcott and Hort, *Notes*, 28–51, Streeter, 333–60, C. S. C. Williams, 40–5.

Notes. E 229 is the Armenian MS discovered at Edschmiadzin and dated A.D. 989 which contains the disputed verses but with the rubric *Ariston Eritzu* ('Of the Presbyter Ariston'). Cf. F. C. Burkitt, *EB*, iv, col. 5011. Just = Justin Martyr (ii). 099 (vii). 0112 (vii).

[1] Streeter, 336, speaks of the Shorter Ending as 'obviously an attempt by some early editor to heal the gaping wound' and as 'additional evidence for a text that ended with ἐφοβοῦντο γάρ.'

16. *Lk. ii. 5*

εμνηστευμενη αυτω ℵ B C D L W 1 565 700 a e f r syᵖ sa bo
Tat: γυναικι αυτου b c aur sy⁸: εμνηστευμενη αυτω
γυναικι (A) Δ Θ fam. 13 28 ff² l q vg *s*.

This example illustrates the possibility that a less well
attested reading may sometimes be original. The third
reading combines the other two and so testifies to the
existence of both. It can hardly be original. Of the first
two readings transcriptional probability favours the second.
'Betrothed' appears to be an earlier modification under the
influence of i. 27 and in the interest of the doctrine of the
Virgin Birth. In point of fact the reading 'his wife' does not
compromise that doctrine and it is probable that the
marriage took place before the journey was undertaken.
The reading has the strong support of Western, Caesarean,
and Antiochian MSS. The first reading is predominantly
Alexandrian, but is well supported by MSS belonging to the
other families. The case is manifestly one in which intrinsic
and transcriptional probability is the decisive issue. So
Creed, 33, Easton, 22, Klostermann, 35, Taylor, *op. cit.*,
32f; but on the other side see Plummer, 53, and C. S. C.
Williams, *op. cit.*, 29. Williams suggests that it is at least as
probable a view (as the explanation given above) that
γυναικι was added by some who imagined that it was more
proper for Joseph to have had Mary as his wife on a journey
than as his espoused, and that once the addition was made,
the conflated 'espoused wife' would follow easily enough.

17. *Lk. xxii. 19b–20*

το υπερ υμων διδομενον . . . εκχυννομενον Pᵗ⁵ Unc. *omn.*
(except D) min. *omn.* c f q r² aur vg bo sa arm aeth Marc Just
Tat (?): Om D a b d e ff² i l (sy⁸ ᶜ): 19a, 17f, b e: 19, 17, 18
syᶜ sy⁸ (with small additions): Om 17f syᵖ.

This important reading is selected in spite of its difficulty
and the wide diversity of opinion among textual critics in

order to illustrate the problems which it raises. The passage is the most important of the 'Western non-interpolations' Westcott and Hort enclose in double brackets in Lk. xxii and xxiv. They point out that the only motive for its omission as a corruption would be a perception of the double reference to the Cup, but that this explanation involves the extreme improbability that the most familiar form of the Words of Institution (cf. 1 Cor. xi. 24f) were omitted while the vaguer words peculiar to Luke were retained. Cf. *Notes*, 63. This is a strong argument and it has exerted great influence upon textual critics.

In recent years, however, the opposite view has been widely taken especially on the Continent, with strong support by a number of British scholars, including F. G. Kenyon and S. C. E. Legg. C. S. C. Williams writes, 'It would seem that the case for the shorter text championed by Nestle, J. Weiss, Loisy, Westcott and Hort, and Burkitt, has been met'. J. Jeremias, who supports the longer text, gives a list of twenty-two continental scholars who take the same view.

There is no doubt that the originality of 19*b*–20 is strongly attested, being found in all MSS except Western and Syriac authorities, in many versions and second century Patristic writers. It may have been omitted for the reason suggested by Westcott and Hort, to remove the second Cup by those who failed to appreciate the difficulty thus produced by the consequent order Cup-Bread. Jeremias prefers the view that the intention is to keep the Eucharist from profanation as a secret, and this explanation, though speculative, is strongly based. In any case it must be recognized that Luke used two different sources in 15–18 and 19–20 and H. Schürmann has powerfully argued on linguistic grounds that 19–20 is not based on Mark (except 20*b*) or 1 Cor. xi. 23–5, but on a third early liturgical source.[1] The case against the Lukan authorship of 19*b*–20 is maintained

---

[1] Professor Jeremias strongly re-enforces his argument in the third edition of his *Die Abendmahlsworte Jesu* (1960) in a new chapter

by G. D. Kilpatrick, who says 'the abruptness of the ending (19*a*) is deliberate in order to preserve the *arcanum* of the rite'.

It will be seen that much remains to be done before one can speak of the original text of Luke with confidence. British scholars in particular do not find it easy to resist the arguments of Westcott and Hort. It is significant, however, that the problem is being increasingly attacked from all sides, textual, historical, linguistic, and exegetical.

For further study of Lk. xxii. 19*b*–20 see Westcott and Hort, *Notes*, 63f; M. Goguel, *The Life of Jesus*, (1933), 458–60; F. Cirlot, *The Early Eucharist* (1939), 241ff; F. G. Kenyon and S. C. E. Legg, *The Ministry and the Sacraments* (ed. R. Dunkerley, 1937), 272ff; G. D. Kilpatrick, *The Journal of Theological Studies*, xlvii (1946), 49–56; P. Benoit, *The Journal of Theological Studies*, xlix (1948), 145–7; C. S. C. Williams, *op. cit.*, (1951), 47–51; J. Jeremias, *op. cit.*, (1955), 87–106; H. Schürmann, *Der Einsetzungsbericht* Lk. xxii. 19–20 (1955).

18. *Lk. xxii. 43f* (The Agony and Bloody Sweat)

ωφθη δε αυτω . . . καταβαινοντες επι την γην *habent* ℵ* D L Θ 0171 fam. 1 157 it vg arm aeth sy^c p Tat Just Iren Hipp: *om* P^75 ℵ^a A B W fam. 13 579 826 *al* f sy^s sa bo^pt Marc Clem Or.

If we had to judge this reading by the textual evidence alone, we should probably decide in favour of the omission of 43f, for the combined witness of ℵ^a, B W, fam. 13, sy^s, and the second-century Patristic writers is very strong. But

entitled 'The Influence of Worship on the Tradition of the Eucharistic Texts' in which he gives many examples of esoteric teaching in late Judaism and primitive Christianity. It will be noticed that both Professor Kilpatrick and Professor Jeremias recognize the motive of concealment from profane eyes, the former as regards the Shorter Text ending with 19*a*, the latter in favour of the Longer Text ending with xxii. 20. Both agree that 19f is not Lucan in diction and style, but Professor Jeremias explains this as due to the use by Luke of a liturgical text.

we should do so with misgivings, for the evidence for the passage is also strong and early. Westcott and Hort, influenced by B and their unwillingness to admit doctrinal considerations, bracket the passage as a 'Western interpolation', and explain it as a fragment from oral or written tradition; but they say that these verses and the first sentence of xxiii. 34 may safely be called 'the most precious among the remains of this evangelic tradition which were rescued from oblivion by the scribes of the second century', *Notes*, 67. But since their day opinion has steadily mounted in favour of the genuineness of the passage. Apparently, as Epiphanius suggests, it caused serious perplexity to some orthodox persons as seemingly derogatory to the full divinity of Christ. 'Presumably,' writes Streeter, 'it seemed beneath the dignity of the Uncreated Word Incarnate to evince such a degree of πάθος; and still more to require a created angel as a comforter,' *op. cit.*, 137. See also Goguel, *The Life of Jesus*, 493; C. S. C. Williams, *op.cit.*, 6–8; J. M. Creed, 273; A. R. C. Leaney, 273. Harnack points out that the vocabulary and style are Lucan.

Notes. 0171 (iv). Hipp = Hippolytus 234. Marc = Marcion *c.* 150.

19. *Lk. xxiii. 34a*

ο δε Ιησους ελεγεν, Πατερ, αφες αυτοις· ου γαρ οιδασιν τι ποιουσιν *habent* ℵ* A L D^c fam. 1 fam. 13 565 700 *al pler* c e vg sy^(c)p arm Marc Tat Iren Clem Or Eus: *om* P^75 ℵ^c B D* W Θ 38 435 579 a b d sy^s sa bo^ht

Another of Westcott and Hort's 'Western interpolations'. They think that the verse would not have been dropped out if it had been part of the original text. 'We cannot doubt,' they say, 'that it comes from an extraneous source.' At the same time, however, they affirm, 'Few verses of the Gospels bear in themselves a surer witness to the truth of what they record than this first of the Words from the Cross,' *Notes*, 68.

In the main commentators agree with the judgement of
Westcott and Hort. J. Rendel Harris suggested that the
verse might have been deleted by some Christian of the
second century who found it hard to believe that God
could or ought to have forgiven the Jews. Streeter, *op. cit.*,
138f, speaks with favour of this suggestion, and says that the
claim of these words to be an authentic part of the Third
Gospel deserves serious consideration, but he does not say
more. Creed, 286, says, 'The omission of a prayer so sub-
lime and so Christ-like seems less probable than its insertion.'
Easton, 348, says that evidence for omission 'seems to be
conclusive'. Leaney, 284, says that the words of the prayer
may be due to Luke, but this opinion is unlikely in view of
the Evangelist's fidelity in reproducing his sources (cf.
Cadbury, *The Style and Literary Method of Luke*, 124).
On the whole it would appear that the genuineness of the
prayer is highly probable, but that its place in the text of
Lk. is uncertain. Cf. A. B. Bruce, *Expositor's Greek Testament*, i. (1897), 639.

20. *Jn. i. 13*

οι ουκ . . . εγεννηθησαν unc. *omn.* min *omn.*: ουκ . . . εγενν.
D a: *non (qui non* b Iren[lat]) . . . *natus est* b Just (?) Iren
Tert: οι ουκ εγεννηθη (*sic*) sy[c] [vid]

The MS evidence is overwhelmingly in favour of the
plural reading, which agrees with τοις πιστευουσιν in
verse 12 and the general sense of the passage. The singular
reading is purely Western and, as the Patristic evidence
shows, as early as the second century. Its origin is due
to doctrinal motives. It introduces a reference to the
Virgin Birth, which is not otherwise mentioned in the Gospel
of John. Cf. J. H. Bernard, 17, C. K. Barrett, 137, C. S. C.
Williams, 30f. Lagrange, 19, says it is a decisive argument
in favour of the spiritual generation of the children of God
that this idea is important in the thought of the author of
the Gospel and I Jn.

21. *Jn. i.* 18

μονογ. Θεος P⁶⁶ P⁷⁵ ℵ* B C L sy^{p h mg} bo Iren^{pt} Or Jer: ο μον.
Θ. ℵ^c 33 Cl^{pt}: ο μον. Υιος A W Θ *al. pler* fam. 1 fam. 13 *al.
plur.* it vg sy^c sa Cl^{pt} Ir^{pt} Tert Eus Chr.

The evidence for μονογ. Θεος is now further supported
by Pap. Bodmer II (P⁶⁶). It is the more difficult reading
and is preferred by Westcott and Hort and Nestle. Cf.
also Bernard, 31; Lagrange, 27; Howard, 479. Θεος
is without the article and with the following words may be
rendered, 'He who is in the bosom of the Father, only-
begotten, divine' (Howard). The change to Υιος is intelligible,
and Barrett, 141, thinks it should be read in view of the
words which follow, but this is how a copyist who found
Θεος difficult may have argued. Probably Θεος should be read.

22. *Jn. iii. 13*

ο ων εν τω ουρανω *habent* A Δ Θ fam. 1 fam. 13 579 *al. pler.* it
vg sy^(c) p bo: ο ων εκ του -νου 0141 sy^s: *om* P⁶⁶ ℵ B L W
et al. 33 sa bo^{pt}.

Scholars hesitate between the view that the passage is a
gloss (WH, 75, Bernard, 112, Howard, 508) or is original
(Hoskyns, 235; Lagrange, 'Nous lisons non sans hésitation,'
80; Barrett, 178). Bernard concedes that if it is original, it
is not easy to account for its omission, since it contains no
doctrine different from that of the Prologue and adds nothing
to the argument. The MSS which omit the phrase are mainly
Alexandrian, and those which attest it are Byzantine,
Caesarean, Western, and Antiochian. If it is an interpreta-
tive gloss, it must have been added at an early date, and
perhaps on the whole it should be accepted.

Notes. 0141 (x)

23. *Jn. iii. 25*

Ιουδαιου ℵ^c A B W 28 *et pler.* sy^{p h} Nonn.: -δαιων P⁶⁶ ℵ*
Θ fam. 1 fam. 13 *al* it vg sy^c sa bo Or ϛ.

Both readings are well attested. The singular is adopted by WH, RV, and RSV. The plural is usual in Jn and probably for this reason $Iov\delta a\iota ov$ deserves preference.

It has been conjectured that neither reading is origina and that $I\eta\sigma ov$ or τov $I\eta\sigma ov$ or $\tau\omega v$ $I\eta\sigma ov$ should be read, the dispute being between the disciples of John and Jesus or His disciples. This suggestion is attractive, but it is without support in the manuscript tradition.

Cf. Bernard, 130, Howard, 515, Barrett, 184. Lagrange, 93, says that $Iov\delta a\iota ov$ 'se recommande absolument par sa rareté'. Barrett takes the same view.

Notes. Nonn = Nonnus iv–v.

24. *Jn. iv. 1*

o $Kv\rho\iota o\varsigma$ P⁶⁶ A B C L W fam. 13 28 700 *al pler* f q δ sy⁸ sa: o $I\eta\sigma ov\varsigma$ ℵ D Θ fam. 1 *al* a b c e ff² l syᶜ ᴾ bo

This example is interesting in view of its bearing on the Evangelist's theology. Each reading is well attested, especially the former. But, apparently, John restricts the use of o $Kv\rho\iota o\varsigma$ to the Resurrection period, for in all the three passages in which it appears before chapter xx (iv. 1, vi. 23, xi. 2) this reading is open to textual and critical objections. Cf. Bernard, 132. Probably, then, o $I\eta\sigma ov\varsigma$ should be read.

Notes. δ Latin of Δ

25. *Jn. v. 3b–4*

3b, 4 (after $\xi\eta\rho\omega v$) om P⁶⁶ P⁷⁵ ℵ B C* D W 33 157 f l q vg (WW) syᶜ: $+\pi a\rho a\lambda v\tau\iota\kappa\omega v$ (after $\xi\eta\rho\omega v$) D a b j l r¹: $+\epsilon\kappa\delta\epsilon\chi o\mu\epsilon v\omega v$ $\tau\eta v$ τov $v\delta a\tau o\varsigma$ $\kappa\iota v\eta\sigma\iota v$ Aᶜ D W Θ fam. 1 fam. 13 *pler* it vg syᴾ Tert Ambr Chr: $+(v. 4)$ $a\gamma\gamma\epsilon\lambda o\varsigma$ $\gamma a\rho$ ... $\kappa a\tau\epsilon\iota\chi\epsilon\tau o$ $v o\sigma\eta\mu a\tau\iota$ A L Θ Ψ fam. 1 fam. 13 *pler* it vg syᴾ Tert

Lagrange, 134, describes the problem as a *Question textuelle célèbre*. There can be little doubt that the shorter text is original. The purpose of the additional readings is to explain the man's statement (*v. 7*) that he had no one to put him into the pool when the water was troubled: another

stepped down before him.   It will be observed that the
additions are predominantly, though not exclusively,
Western and Caesarean and, as the testimony of Tertullian
suggests, were made in the second century, and probably in
view of their wide diffusion early in that century.   The
linguistic evidence is also against their genuineness.   Several
words are non-Johannine.   Cf. Bernard, 229.   For the
association of angels with the mysterious powers of water
see Apoc. xvi. 5.

For smaller variants in the text of *v.* 4 see Nestle.

Notes.   j Saretianus (v–vi).

26. *Jn. vii. 53–viii. 11 (Pericope Adulterae)*

Habent D 28 700 *et al. pler.* b* c e ff² j l^c z vg sy^{pal} Ambr
Ambst Aug Jer: *post* vii. 36 225: *post* xxi. 24 1 1583:
post Lk. xxi. 38 fam. 13: *om* P⁶⁶ P⁷⁵ ℵ B W Θ 22 33 157 565
al a b^c f l* q sy sa bo arm geo goth Ir Cl^{vid} Or Tert Cypr
Nonn

The objections to the genuineness of the section in Jn
are conclusive.   The combination of P⁶⁶, B, Θ, and the
Syriac (except sy^{pal}), supported by many Old Latin MSS
and the testimony of important Greek and Latin Fathers, is
especially strong.   The authorities which attest the passage
are almost entirely Western or of late and inferior standing.
Moreover, as in the case of v. 3*b*–4, the vocabulary and style
are non-Johannine.   One must conclude that it is a late
Western insertion derived from some traditional source.
Westcott and Hort conjecture that the source was the
Gospel according to the Hebrews or the *Expositions of the
Lord's Oracles* of Papias.   In any case it is probably a
fragment of authentic tradition.   See the full discussions of
Bernard, 715–21;   Lagrange, 221–6;   Hoskyns, 673–85;
Westcott and Hort, 82–8;   Barrett, 490–3.

Notes.   z Aureus (viii).   Ambst = Ambrosiaster (commentary on
St. Paul) iv.

27. *Jn. xix. 29*

υσσωπω] υσσω 476*

This example raises the interesting question of the value of a conjecture supported by a single late MS against the rest of the textual tradition.

A bunch of hyssop would not be stiff enough to raise a wet sponge to the lips of a crucified man. Mk. xv. 36 mentions a reed (καλάμῳ) which is much more suitable. In the sixteenth century Joachim Camerarius conjectured that the original reading was υσσω (Lat. *pilum*, a javelin) and subsequently this reading was actually found in the eleventh century minuscule 476. The conjecture has won considerable favour (cf. Bernard, 640, Lagrange, 496, Howard, 784f). Against this suggestion it has been pointed out that hyssop was used in the observance of the Passover and may have been deliberately introduced into his narrative by the Evangelist in view of his desire to set forth Christ as the true Paschal Lamb (So Bauer, Goguel, Loisy, cf. Barrett, 460). Cf. Ex. xii. 22, where it is enjoined that the Israelites were to take a bunch of hyssop and, after dipping it in the blood in the basin, were to strike the lintel and the door posts of the house. This suggestion is attractive and may be sound, but seems strained in view of the entirely different purposes implied in Ex. xii. 22 as compared with Jn. xix. 29. No doubt conjectures are to be received with caution, even when supported by late MS evidence, in view of the wealth of the MS tradition, but they cannot be neglected, especially when as in the present case they are readily explained by a primitive misreading of the original text and supply it with a greater verisimilitude.

28. *Acts xv. 20*

και της πορνειας] om. P⁴⁵ aethᵖᵗ | και πνικτου] om D d g Iren Ephr Ambr Ambst Aug | αιματος]+και οσα μη θελουσιν εαυτοις γινεσθαι ετεροις μη ποιειτε (ποιειν 1739 *pc* Iren) D 69ᵐᵍ 1739 *pc* d sa Iren Eus Ephr.

This passage is part of the Apostolic decree which laid
down the conditions under which the Gentiles might have
table fellowship with Jewish Christians. See also xv. 29
and xxi. 25. It bears upon the question whether the four
restrictions laid down, the pollution of idols, fornication,
that which is strangled, and blood, were part of a food law
(as in the β text) or (with the omission of 'that which is
strangled' and the addition of the Golden Rule) constituted
a moral code (as in the δ text). The reference to fornication
seems strange in a food law and it is not surprising that a
few MSS omit πορνειας. On the other side 'that which
is strangled' is out of place in a moral code and the
Golden Rule even in a negative form is in harmony with
it.

It will be seen that most of the authorities which omit
και πνικτου and insert the Golden Rule are Western, with
some Eastern support. It is widely agreed that this text
(the δ text) is the result of an intentional revision, and that
priority should be given to the β text. Cf. F. F. Bruce,
299f, and for a detailed study of the alternative explanations
cf. K. Lake, *The Beginnings of Christianity*, vol. v, 204-12.
The question at issue is 'the practical one of social inter-
course between Jewish and Gentile Christians (including
joint participation in the Lord's Supper), and of concessions
which Gentiles are to be invited to make to avoid scandalizing
their weaker Jewish brethren', (Bruce, 300).

29. Rom. v. 1

εχομεν אc Bc F G P 0220*vid* vg *pc* sa Did Epiph Cl: εχωμεν
א* A B* C D K L 69 1739 *pm* it vg sy arm aeth bo Marc Or
Chr Ambst

This example illustrates the possibility that an inferior
reading may have strong claims to be considered original.

The subjunctive has very strong support and is read by
Westcott and Hort and Souter and is followed in the RV

text, 'let us have peace with God'. The indicative, 'we have', is preferred by Nestle, and is read by the AV, the RV margin, and the RSV. The commentators are divided, with perhaps a growing preference for the indicative. Sanday and Headlam, 120, come down on the side of the subjunctive, 'let us enjoy peace', but point out that the vowels o and ω were frequently interchanged (cf. Gal. vi. 10, I Cor. xv. 49), and they quote the opinion of Scrivener, 'inference not exhortation is the Apostle's purpose'. Cf. Findlay, 821. On the other side, Denney, 623, Boylan, 75f, J. Knox, 451f, Barrett, 102, and others, defend the indicative.

Why is the indicative preferred? Partly because of the point made by Scrivener, that Paul is describing the results of justification, but also because it is now recognized that in spoken Greek there was little or no difference in sound between the two vowels. An error may go back to the hearing of Tertius, the original amanuensis. Cf. Moulton, *Grammar*, i. 110, 247, ii. 74. This possibility strongly re-enforces the argument based on Paul's apparent purpose, and makes it possible, against the overwhelming textual support for εχωμεν, to accept the rendering, 'we have peace with God'.

Notes. D (in St Paul) =D₂. F=F₂. G=G₂. P=P₂. K Mosquensis (ix). L=L₂ Angelicus (ix). 0220 (iv). Did=Didymus *c.* 393. Epiph=Epiphanius 403.

30. *I Cor. iv. 6*

ινα εν ημιν μαθητε το Μη (μη *om.* D E) υπερ α γεγραπται, ινα μη εις υπερ του ενος φυσιουσθε (φυσιουσθαι ℵ*c et al*) κατα του ετερου] + φρονειν (*post* γεγραπται) 33 *pm* sy *s*

The possibility of *textual* glosses cannot be excluded (as distinct from simple conjectures) where good editors think that the text as we have it is corrupt, and it will be of interest to describe one of these in I Cor. iv. 6, even though a confident judgement is not possible.

The RV rendering of the opening words is 'that in us ye

H

might learn not *to go* beyond the things which are written . . .'
(where 'to go' is understood and therefore printed in italics).
It is generally agreed that the phrase refers to the Scriptures,
but the commentators are obviously embarrassed to know
what precisely is meant. A. S. Peake, 836, says, 'The text
is probably corrupt,' and J. Moffatt in a footnote in his
Translation observes, 'The text and the meaning of the
phrase . . . are beyond recovery.' In these circumstances
W. F. Howard has suggested that the words should be
regarded as a *textual gloss* (*ET*, xxxiii. (1922), 479f). The
Dutch scholar Baljon suggested that a scribe, who found
μη missing inserted it over the εἶς (written in the numerical
form ā) and added the comment τὸ μὴ ὑπὲρ ā γέγραπται,
and Bousset made a similar suggestion referring to the final
α in ἵνα. J. Weiss, after quoting Baljon's 'very clever conjecture', suggested that the marginal gloss read ā γέγραπται'
˙ ἕνα μὴ εἶς, i.e. 'the ā stands in the text; read it as
ἕνα not εἶς' (or possibly ἕνα ἢ εἶς, i.e. 'how is it to be
resolved, ἕνα or εἶς?'). He further suggested that the
infin. φυσιοῦσθαι should be read and the passage translated,
'that in us ye may learn not to be puffed up one on behalf
of one (teacher) against the other'.

It is perhaps not surprising that these suggestions, any of
which would explain the text, have not been adopted by
commentators, since no direct textual evidence can be quoted
in their favour, but whether this objection is adequate
seems doubtful. To suggest that some proverb may be in
mind is a case of grasping at straws.

Almost alone among British commentators Howard writes
in the *Abingdon Bible Commentary* (1929, p. 1176f) 'The five
Greek words translated "not to go beyond the things which
are written" are almost certainly a marginal gloss. . . . Their
intrusion reduces the text to nonsense, from which no expository ingenuity has ever drawn a satisfactory meaning.
Without these words the text states, "I have used these
metaphors in writing of Apollos and myself on your account,

to show how absurd it is for any of you to pride himself on his party loyalty to one of us by disparaging the other." '

Notes. D = D₂. E = E₃ Sangermanensis (ix–x).

31. *Gal. ii. 5*

οις ουδε P⁴⁶ ℵ A B Dᶜ G *pl* 33 f g vg bo arm aeth ς: ουδε Marc Ephr *Graeci apud* Ambst: *om* D* d e vg(1) Ir¹ᵃᵗ Tert Ambst Pelag | τη υποταγη om. P⁴⁶

Textual criticism sometimes has an important bearing on historical questions. The question of the circumcision of Titus furnishes a good example. Was he, or was he not, circumcised?

Kirsopp Lake, *The Beginnings of Christianity*, v. 196–9, is inclined to think that he was, but he says that a verdict of 'not proven' ought to be returned. Burkitt, *Christian Beginnings*, 118, speaks more positively. 'Who can doubt,' he asks, 'that it was the knife which really did circumcise Titus that has cut the syntax of Gal. ii. 3–5 to pieces?' It may be questioned, however, if the variants in verse 5 are not grammatical emendations. The problem is whether we are, or are not, to omit the negative. Klostermann and Zahn are on the one side in omitting the negative, and Tischendorf, Tregelles, Westcott and Hort, J. Weiss, the RV, and the RSV are on the other. So most modern interpreters.

Burton, 85, thinks the evidence against οις ουδε 'is not sufficiently strong to overcome the strong preponderance in its favour, or the improbability that any one would have introduced the anacoluthic οἷς'. This appears to be the best view to take. Not only is οις ουδε very strongly attested, but the phrase which follows, 'that the truth of the Gospel might continue with you', is not intelligible if Paul yielded to the demand that Titus should be circumcised. Probably ουδε was omitted in the second century in many Western MSS. Why the negative was omitted we cannot say. It may have been omitted by inadvertance or because verse 3,

'But not even Titus who was with me, being a Greek, was compelled to be circumcised,' was misinterpreted to mean that in fact he was circumcised.

Notes. G = G₃ Boernerianus (ix). Pelag = Pelagius iv–v. *Graeci apud* Ambst = Greek MSS according to Ambrosiaster.

32. *Eph. i. 1*

εν Εφεσω א^c B^c A D G *pl* it vg sy *s*: *om* P⁴⁶ א* B* 424^c 1739 Marc (Tert) Or Bas

The absence of these words from א*, B*, the writings of Marcion, Origen, and Basil, and now P⁴⁶, is one of the strong arguments by which it is maintained (*a*) that the Epistle is a circulatory letter, or (*b*) that it is of non-Pauline authorship. For the various arguments, linguistic, stylistic, literary, historical, and doctrinal cf. J. A. Robinson, 292–5, T. K. Abbott, i–ix, 2f, C. L. Mitton, *The Epistle to the Ephesians* (1951).

33. *Heb. ii. 9*

χαριτι Θεου unc. *omn* (except M) it *et* vg *omn* sy^h: χωρις Θεου M 424^c 1739 sy^p (3) Or^{pt} Eus Theod^{mopsu} *codd. apud* Jer Ambr

This dogmatic variant is of much interest because of its bearing on the history of the text. Moffatt points out that the meaning of χωρις Θεου may be (i) 'forsaken by God' (cf. Mk. xv. 34), (ii) 'apart from his divinity', (iii) taken with παντος 'die for everyone (everything?) except God', which was Origen's view, and suggests that only i or iii are tenable. The fact that the reading was popular among the Nestorians, he thinks, 'tended to compromise χωρις in the eyes of the later church', and suggests that long associations render it difficult for a modern scholar to do justice to it, but on the whole he favours the view that at some early stage there must have been a corruption of the text, which cannot be explained upon the available data. If χωρις Θεου is secondary, some primitive scribe may have written the words in the

margin as a gloss upon παντος or even after ουδεν . . .
ανυποτακτον (verse 8). Westcott also explains the phrase
as a scribal gloss, but Harnack thinks the phrase belongs to
the primitive text. Cf. Moffatt, 26f, Westcott, 60–2, Peake,
102f.

Transcriptional probability may be held to favour χωρις,
and the evidence of the Fathers, especially Origen, carries
the reading back to the third and probably the second
century. It is also possible that it was read by many more
MSS than those in which it now appears. The hypothesis of a
very early gloss explains the facts, especially if it was a
comment on the closing words of verse 8. χαριτι Θεου is in
harmony with the context and probably should be read,
attested as it is by MSS of all families.

Notes. M (Codex Ruber) contains fragments of 1 and 2 Cor.
and Hebrews (ix). Theod^{mopsu} = Theodore of Mopsuestia iv–v.
codd. apud Jer Ambr = codices according to Jerome and Ambrose.

34. *Heb. iv. 2*

συνκεκερασμενος (-κεκραμ- *pc* ς) ℵ d vg^{s, cl} sy^p sa (2) Lcf:
-κεκερασμεμους (-κεκραμενους P *pm*) P^{13, 46} A B D* 69 *al*
vg^w sy^h bo sa (3) Chr Theod^{mopsu} Aug

This passage illustrates the influence of exegesis on textual
decisions. The singular, though less strongly attested, is
accepted by some of the best commentators, the plural being
explained as an assimilation to εκεινους. Moffatt, 51, takes
this view and translates the passage, 'because it (ο λογος
της ακοης, "the message they heard") did not meet with
faith in the hearers.' His objection to the plural ('since they
did not mix with the believing hearers') is the absence of any
allusion to the faithful minority (Caleb and Joshua). Westcott, 93f, 110f, also thinks that συνκεκερασμενος appears
to offer the least difficulty. So also Peake, 123, who takes
the meaning to be that, in the case of those who heard it,
the word was not mixed with faith, did not meet with a
believing response, and thus remained unprofitable.

The question arises how far good exegesis can stand against a variant reading so strongly attested by important uncials and P[13] and P[46], although it may be argued that transcriptional probability favours the reading in the singular.   It may be recalled that Westcott and Hort, *Notes*, 129, marked the passage as probably containing a primitive corruption, although, as we have seen, Westcott in his commentary comes down on the side of συνκεκερασμενος.

Notes. vg[s] = the Sixtine Vulgate of 1590. vg[cl] = the Clementine Vulgate of 1592. vg[w] = Wordsworth and White's text (see p. 29). Lcf = Lucifer 371. P = P₂ (ix). D = D₂ (vi).

Although the passages examined above discuss special points, they may easily leave the impression, mentioned at the beginning of this chapter, that much of the text of the New Testament is uncertain, since experts differ so greatly. In a measure this uncertainty exists, and is an impressive warning against the claim that the Bible is verbally inspired. But the degree of uncertainty is small when it is measured proportionately in the New Testament as a whole.   Westcott and Hort estimated that the proportion of words virtually accepted as raised above doubt is not less, on a rough computation, than seven-eighths of the whole, and that the remaining one-eighth consists for the most part of changes in the order of words and other comparative trivialities.   In their opinion the words still subject to doubt amount to only one-sixtieth of the entire New Testament.   'We desire to make it clearly understood beforehand', they wrote, 'how much of the New Testament stands in no need of a textual critic's labours.'[1] Probably their estimate still stands, for as we have pointed out,[2] while new discoveries of MSS solve some problems, they also raise others.

It would be easy to draw the opposite inference, and to conclude that textual criticism may safely be left to the small band of experts.   But this hasty conclusion ignores the value

---

[1] *Op. cit.*, 3.   [2] P. 67

of grappling objectively with New Testament problems to-day in a period when subjective criticism appears to be excessive. Textual criticism is an objective scientific study. For this reason, I believe, it is a tonic in times of religious depression, and a source of confidence in the solidity of Scripture testimony.

INDEX OF SCRIPTURE PASSAGES

INDEX OF PROPER NAMES

PRINTED IN GREAT BRITAIN
BY ROBERT MACLEHOSE AND CO. LTD
THE UNIVERSITY PRESS, GLASGOW